SOMETIMES ROUGH ROADS
LEAD TO RIGHT PLACES

Detours

Clark Cothern

Multnomah Publishers *Sisters, Oregon*

DETOURS
Published by Multnomah Publishers, Inc.
© 1999 by Clark Cothern
International Standard Book Number: 1-57673-286-X
Design by D² DesignWorks
Cover photograph by Bernhard Michael Schmid/Photonica

Printed in the United States of America

Most Scripture quotations are from:
The Holy Bible, New International Version (NIV)
© 1973, 1984 by International Bible Society,
used by permission of Zondervan Publishing House.

Multnomah is a registered trademark of Multnomah Publishers, Inc.

The colophon is a trademark of Multnomah Publishers, Inc.

For information
Multnomah Publishers, Inc.
Post Office Box 1720 • Sisters, Oregon 97759

Library of Congress Cataloging-in-Publication Data:
Cothern, Clark.
    Detours: sometimes rough roads lead to right places/Clark
Cothern.
        p.cm. Includes bibliographical references.
    ISBN 1-57673-286-X (alk. paper) 1. consolation. 2. Christian
    life. 3. Suffering-Religious aspects-Christianity. I. Title.
BV4909.C68   1999   98-37402
248.4–dc21   CIP

99 00 01 02 03 04 05 06 — 10 9 8 7 6 5 4 3 2 1

To my parents
Gaylon Clark Cothern
and Fayly Hardcastle Cothern
gifted guides on the journey
courageous fellow travelers
and two of the most purpose-filled people I know

Contents

Acknowledgments

The journey on the road to this book was filled with a few detours of its own. I am eternally indebted to those who made it a purpose-filled process:

Our Trinity faith family, with their amazing support and outreaching vision.

Those who let me tell their true stories, with their trust and bravery.

Deb Blohm and Mary Schaap at Sounds of Light Book Store, with their servant spirits and practical help.

Jimmie and Tina Avery, with their ministry to the technologically challenged. Ed Gore, Ron Potter, and Chris Pollard, with their collective wisdom and enthusiasm-producing encouragement.

George and Marilyn "Mom and Dad" Castle, with their travel trailer hideaway for frazzled sons-in-law facing blood pressure-raising deadlines.

Kathey Cothern, with her continued love, courageous persistence, and solid support.

Katheryn, Clark III, and Callie Cothern, with their profound love, childlike faith, and indescribable joy.

Joy "the most patient wife in the world" Cothern, with her multiple ministry gifts and her giant healer's heart.

The Multnomah family, with their continued commitment to ministry and humble professionalism. And Larry Libby, editor, mentor, friend, with his teacher's talents and shepherd's soul.

CHAPTER ONE

Detoured from Oz

Willing the approaching traffic light to stay green, I asked the Munchkin sitting next to me to check on the injured Tin Woodman in the back of the pickup.

I glanced at the speedometer as we hurtled through the intersection under an amber light. Sixty-five miles an hour. Crazy teenager. If I got a ticket, my insurance rates would go through the roof—and so would my dad.

A thickset nurse in her midfifties lifted her eyes above her reading glasses as a tall, skinny Scarecrow and a short, petite Munchkin helped a clanking, aluminum Tin Woodman into the receiving area. Based on her unflinching reaction to our arrival, I had no doubt that this lady had seen it all. Just another day in the life at the ER.

Arching her left eyebrow, she invited an explanation.

Already in costume, I couldn't help hamming it up a bit. "Dorothy and the Cowardly Lion will be along soon," I explained. "They got stuck at a red light. But don't worry, there are no lions, tigers, or bears."

Our woodman made a strange sound—something between a wheeze and a groan—trying in vain to reach behind himself and grab his back. Bound by the aluminum sheeting encircling his upper body, he couldn't get it done. Moaning in real agony, he clanked to the floor and began rolling back and forth, sounding like two dozen soup cans bouncing along behind a wedding limousine.

At this, the stoic nurse sprang into action. "Oh my," she said, snatching off her glasses and racing to the Tin Man's side.

"Tell him to stop the jokes," he said, gesturing weakly in my direction. "They're *killing* me."

This particular detour began as most detours do.

Unexpectedly.

There we were, merrily rolling along toward a successful opening night performance of *The Wizard of Oz* when CLANK, a simple misstep sent us careening off the yellow brick road. Instead, we found ourselves racing down the hot Phoenix pavement to Maryvale Samaritan Hospital. To see a nurse...about a Tin Man.

Up to that point, dress rehearsal had gone relatively well, except for the fact that yours truly—a.k.a. Scarecrow—went completely blank about halfway through the first act. My lapse left a gap in the dialogue the size of the Emerald City, but with the aid of a whispered cue, I managed to ad lib my way back into the correct scene. Just in time, too. We were about to encounter Her Nastiness, the Wicked Witch of the West.

After the recovered cue, the lights dimmed and the stage crew hauled on ropes that unfurled a new backdrop, transforming a two-dimensional cornfield into a cavernous Wizard's hall.

My friend and fellow thespian, Chuck "Tin Man" Sigars, hauled himself and his cumbersome costume into position for the next big scene. Dorothy, the Cowardly Lion, and I were preparing ourselves to shake, rattle, and chatter our requests to a talking head projected on a scrim hovering just above center stage.

Halfway up the three little steps, however, the woodman lost his footing. It was a very easy thing to do, when you consider Chuck couldn't see his silver shoes beneath his bulky metal midsection (a rare cooperative effort between the drama department and the metal shop).

Before any of us could catch him, Chuck fell backward. As though in slow motion I saw him going down, but I couldn't get the signal from my straw-stuffed head to my feet to run over and steady him. I felt brainless and numb as I watched Chuck vainly try to catch himself.

He struck the wooden stage with a crack like thunder, feeling the shock shoot through the nerves of his back and neck like a bolt of lightning. Chuck immediately began arching his back, his muscles wrenched into agonizing knots.

Not knowing how badly he was hurt, we avoided moving his head and neck, fearing we might make things worse. After a brief discussion, we decided the best way to keep him from moving was to leave his costume in place. The only position that seemed to offer a bit of relief to poor Chuck was flat on his back. The very thought of sitting upright sent him into spasms of pain sharper than his ax head.

As we weighed our options, I suggested transporting him to the hospital in my pickup. "We could get him there in five minutes," I reasoned. "It could take fifteen or twenty if we call the paramedics."

Our drama teacher, Rosemary Williams, wasn't so sure. "Are you okay with being moved, Chuck?"

"As long—as they—keep me—flat," he gasped.

It didn't appear he was in any danger of a spinal cord injury—he still had feeling in all his extremities. So I backed my father's 1960 Ford pickup to the loading dock behind the stage entrance, and four crew members slid Chuck carefully across the cement, over the open tailgate, and into the truck.

Chuck was really hurting, and that wasn't funny. But he looked so pitiful sprawled in that pickup bed it was hard to suppress a snicker. It looked for all the world as if we'd stolen the Lumberjack statue from Northern Arizona University up in Flagstaff. Except for the contorted expression on his silver face, he looked more like a mascot than an actor.

He forced a weak smile and tried to breath slowly through his nose, which, with the help of face putty, jutted out about three inches from his face, ending in a funnel-like point with a little hole poked into the end.

Every time someone said something remotely funny (which unfortunately for Chuck was pretty often), he would grimace, arch his back, and groan, trying to reach the elusive muscle which was by now as hard as oak.

"I'll shut the tailgate so you won't slide out and accidentally knock down a telephone pole," I said softly, trying to ease the tension. He started to smile but then grimaced in pain.

Catching myself, I held out my hand palm forward.

"Oops. Sorry, Chuck. Don't laugh."

That did it.

He howled—and then writhed some more. It was neither the time nor the place for healing humor.

His sister Jeannie, the main Munchkin, hopped into the cab next to me, maneuvering her hair carefully through the door opening. Her two long pigtails had been braided around pieces of clothes hanger wire so they stuck way up in the air on each side of her head, curving slightly forward.

A tiny, size-two freshman, Jeannie looked every bit the part of a Lullaby League member. And with me in my straw-shedding outfit, crooked red nose, floppy hat, and burlap-layered face, we sang, "Weeeee're *off* to see the doctor…"

Dorothy, The Wicked Witch, and the Cowardly Lion hopped into a yellow VW Beetle and followed, hoping to help unload our metallic friend, who bumped, clanked, wiggled, and groaned in the back of the truck as I drove north as fast as was safely possible on 59th Avenue toward Indian School Road.

That's the way it is with detours. You're zooming along on a course bound for your destination when suddenly, CLANK. Some outside force beyond your control (be it accident, event, circumstance, or someone else's decision or action) changes your direction. Then off you go down *another* road, one you wouldn't otherwise have traveled.

Those detours in my life, the funny ones, the tragic ones, the perplexing ones, have often led me to places I really wanted to be all along. I just hadn't known how to get there. But God knew all along. Months—and sometimes years—after the fact, I've had to acknowledge His wisdom...and my reluctant gratitude.

Like the lesson I learned from Chuck's fall and our team effort to cart him off to the hospital: *A crisis that causes a detour can also knit people together with the threads of a common purpose and uncommon caring.*

What started out as a simple senior musical presentation ended up as a close-knit family of students. Opening night went well, with Chuck on pain medication and muscle relaxants, and with me at his elbow, watching for any sign that he might be ready to convulse. The entire cast acted with real passion, because we were acting with compassion.

Something happened in that first performance that we had not experienced in rehearsal. Something happened to that group of individual performers that I will never forget.

When we started caring for one another—caring more for the other guy than for grabbing the spotlight for ourselves—we became what we had not been to that point. A team. The individual actors became less significant than the ensemble.

We all felt it. And so did the audience.

None of us would have chosen Chuck's fall as the method by which we learned that lesson, but running through the middle of that detour was a profound truth: *A team of caring people performs better than a collection of individuals, no matter what their talents.*

The audience gave the cast and crew a standing ovation on opening night, again at the Saturday matinee, and on closing night as well. Most observers never knew the pain that had drawn our little company together...but they appreciated the end result.

In the years following that Oz adventure, while riding the roller coaster of emotions that often accompany detours, I have felt shocked, angry, frustrated, frightened, and even downright exasperated. Each side road, each bumpy diversion from the main highway, seemed to be taking me away from the comfortable direction I had originally chosen.

But looking back at those strange deviations from my original course, I have seen that they were often the very routes God had either chosen or allowed. (He hasn't often given me the easy way out, even though I've often prayed for it.) *After* the smoke of the latest crisis has cleared, I've realized again and again that God had been walking alongside me all along, propping me up like a wounded Tin Man, guiding my awkward feet when I couldn't even see the steps ahead of me.

And throughout the journey, He's been trying to capture my attention so He could reveal His purposes—and Himself— more powerfully than if I had stayed on the course I had chosen before the detour.

I've caught myself saying, "I only wish I'd had brains enough to see those purposes and learn those lessons while I was in the *middle* of the detour, instead of having to wait until afterward."

I'd like to think I'm getting better at traveling the detours. I'd like to think that I'm growing more mature in my faith walk, and that I'm learning to recognize the purposes and learn the lessons more quickly.

What I'd really like to do is to recognize a detour the instant it happens, so instead of getting blown off course by the current storm, I can quickly adjust my sails to catch the Spirit's wind and start reciting, "There's no purpose but God's... there's no purpose but God's...."

Maybe you've been down a couple of those unexpected side roads. Perhaps you've been stunned by the solemn voice of the doctor who says, "Please, shut the door behind you...and have a seat."

You might have been jolted awake by the jangle of the phone at 3:30 A.M., and heard the steely voice of a graveyard-shift police officer.

There's a chance that you've experienced, or know someone who has experienced, the lightning strike of divorce papers.

Maybe, just maybe, you're in the midst of a detour right now. The road is rough. The scenery is strange. The landmarks are unfamiliar.

Whatever the detour, whether you've been there or *are* there, I hope you'll discover a renewed sense of purpose by traveling through a few of my detours with me.

At least you'll know you're not alone. If that's the only thing you learn in the following pages, friend, learn that.

In the Bible, the Aramean army once made the mistake of planning their attack on the theory that the God of Israel was only a "god of the hills and not a god of the valleys." Bad idea. He proved—to their destruction—that He was God of all.

Yes, He is Lord of those smooth, wide interstates in your life.

But He is also Lord of the detours.

CHAPTER TWO

Hardcastle's Island

Ha! See there, you knaves," I yelled. "I'm too quick for you, you sluggards!" I swiped at them with my weapon. *Scratch, scratch.* "Take that!" *Scratch.*

On a crisp, cider-smelling, leaf-raking October day I found myself engaged in fierce combat on "the island" in Oak Creek Canyon.

The sounds ricocheted off the walls of the nearby fortress (my grandparents' house): rakes scratching the damp earth, leaves crackling and crunching. The surrounding smells wafted across the battlefield: sycamore bark, pine sap, and other earthy, leafy scents, with an occasional whiff of apple cider and cinnamon drifting from the Crock-Pot on my grandmother's kitchen counter, out through the slightly open window and into the line of fire.

Indulging my senses, I closed my eyes for a moment, drew

in a deep breath through my nose, and thought, *Ah, the life of a warrior.*

The island, to the eyes of a seven-year-old boy, was a vast kingdom, with caves and coves, foxholes and ravines, and a dozen secret hiding places where treasures had been hidden away from evildoers.

In the car, on the way up to Sedona from Phoenix, my father had tried to prepare me for the adventure in Oak Creek. He must have known that my personal purpose for riding with him to Sedona was very different from his purpose. I was willing to endure a boring car ride for two hours because I knew there was a payoff at the end of the trail. When I got to Sedona I could explore, imagine, hike, discover.

In short, I was intending to *play.*

But this time, Dad had something else in mind for me. "Your grandfather is building some cottages on an island," he began.

Just the year before, I had spent languid summer days in the apple and apricot trees and by the creek behind The View Motel. I couldn't imagine anything bigger than the property behind The View.

"Wow, a whole island!" I said.

My father chuckled. I didn't know why, but I had learned to chuckle, too, when he chuckled. Owning your own island was not, in my opinion, a laughing matter, but I chuckled, since it was the socially acceptable thing to do when you wanted your dad to think you knew what was going on.

"He's got a *lot* of work to do," Dad said pointedly, "and he's going to need some help. That's why we're heading up there...to help him."

"Okay," I said, mulling it over. This signaled a major change in plans. That four-letter word, W-O-R-K, had not been on my agenda.

"Your granddaddy and I think you're big enough to help us," Dad went on. "We're countin' on someone who can do a good job—without running off to play every five minutes. Understand?"

Though my head was nodding yes, my mind was thinking, *Rats!* I drew in a deep breath and let out a long sigh, emptying myself of all expectations of fun that day.

"The secret to hard work," Dad was saying, "is to turn work into play. Use your imagination. Make it fun."

Yeah, right. Sounded like one of those lame lines parents use when they're trying to scam you into doing something. Like when my mom used to say with that light, cheery voice, "Let's have a *room-cleaning* party!"

Huh-uh. No sale.

My dad's only purpose was to spoil my fun. I just knew it. He'd probably stayed awake the night before thinking of ways he could make his little boy suffer.

He launched into point number three of his sermon: "The reward for hard work, son, is the sense of accomplishment you get knowing you've done your best. It feels good to be able to look back at what you've done and say, 'That's good. That's the best I can do.'"

Blah, blah, blah. Most of his words were lost on my young ears. I had envisioned castles and moats, bad guys and good guys. Weapons and warriors. And here I was trapped inside a sixty-five-mile-an-hour schoolhouse, receiving a lecture about contributing to something much larger than myself.

Phooey.

He was talking exams and I was wishing for recess.

With my nose pressed against the glass, I stared out the window at the crags and cliffs of what people call Red Rock country, some of God's most amazing scenery in Arizona. I worked at keeping my mind focused on being angry at my dad for forcing me into hard labor, but (in spite of myself) my attitude began to shift along with the shadows of Bell Rock, which loomed larger as we drew near. Try as I might, it was becoming very difficult to maintain my dour disposition.

I imagined my shoulder being tapped by King Arthur's sword. I was to be his squire. My father's words sifted down and mixed with my musings. Seeing my attention drift, he drove the point home one more time. "So we're not going to play. Understand?"

He thought he had a lot of convincing to do, but I'd already accepted my fate. In my mind I set my jaw and tipped my head slowly downward, accepting the responsibility nobly, with appropriate humility.

"Yes, sir," I said.

I wondered if the ruler of this island kingdom would have me joust the evil Black Knight...or perhaps save a damsel or two in distress in a blazing exhibition of swordsmanship.

Sir Clark Cothern wasn't one of those loaf-around do-nothings. Not while evil lurked in the kingdom! I was going to be a warrior, and my commanding officer was reading my orders.

Cool! They must have really thought I was trustworthy to assign a kid destined for third grade the task of protecting the castle on an island from fierce intruders. Most kids would goof off and run around looking for toads and stuff. But I was going to *work*. The last of my sour attitude evaporated like desert dew. In those few moments, I'd made the transformation from *Les Misérables* to *Fantasy Island*.

"There it is." Dad pointed ahead to a dip in the dirt road.

"What?" I asked. I thought he'd spotted a deer or a squirrel. Or maybe a lion or tiger. (I was old enough to know there were no bears here.)

"The island."

"Where?"

"There."

I didn't want to sound completely stupid, but I couldn't help asking, "What island?"

He drove across the dirt that had been piled over three metal culverts, up a slight incline into a tree-covered area, and stopped.

"This," he said, his arms gesturing expansively, "is *it.*"

I looked carefully, but all I saw were trees and a couple of little cinder-block buildings. It wasn't quite as grand in reality as it was in my imagination. But that was okay. My mind would turn it into an enchanted walled city.

In fact…it already had.

One man had purchased this wild territory with money he'd saved from carefully managing a small motel he had built with his own two hands. After a stress-induced ulcer had nearly done him in, this five-foot-one-inch dynamo had built The View Motel as therapy. One man's work is another man's escape, and this energetic man felt rested when he was working with his hands.

The same shoulders that once stooped from the weight of other people's problems now were strong enough to carry an eighty-pound sack of cement. With each nail driven, a burden was driven away. At least in this type of work, he could see a finished product. When you work with people, tangible progress is sometimes hard to find.

He now owned an entire island. What wealth must a man possess to own such an expanse of dirt, trees, boulders, and hiding places? And he had built his island empire one nail at a time, as he had the motel. I knew this man must be both talented and wise to craft a resort on his own island. To his face I called him Granddaddy, but in my adventurous imagination, I referred to him by his real first name, Willard.

Sir Willard the Wise, Lord of Hardcastle Island. (His last name was Hardcastle.)

Handed a stout rake from the royal armory, I worked furiously. To outside eyes it appeared I was merely raking leaves. But I knew differently. I knew that my raking—leaf by leaf—was saving my grandfather's kingdom from evil intruders. The faster I piled the leaves, the sooner I would be saved from their attack. Tiny semicircle fortresses of leaves dotted the landscape as testimony to the quick-thinking defense of a valiant knight. The enemy, confounded and dismayed, circled round and round, looking for an opening.

After two hours of heated battle, Willard backed the leaf-laden truck to the edge of the ravine, with the tailgate hanging over the boulder and cement levee. My father, who was also working with us, hoisted me up over the side of the truck bed just behind the cab, where I began sweeping the collected leaves into the dry creek bed below.

I gasped in awe of the majesty he had already created. An avalanche of rust, gold, yellow, red, and brown leaves cascaded from the back of the faded pink pickup truck, landing on a pile thirty feet wide and twelve feet high. I gazed at the glorious welcome mat that invited courageous knights to leap from the castle tower to safety in the moat below. (Hadn't my father told me that work has its rewards?)

My grandfather had not only swept the entire island clean of the leafy bunkers, but now he had crafted an exhilarating escape route from the lofty heights of the cliff-perched castle into the bowels of the earth. He'd done it again. By his sheer, unflagging persistence, Willard the Wise's stature had achieved monumental proportions.

"He's a worker, isn't he?"

As long as I live, I will never forget those words.

Granddaddy's comment jostled my focus from feverish raking. I pretended not to notice that his words were directed toward my father—and that his raised eyebrow was aimed at me. But as I flicked the last three leaves from the back of the Chevy over the edge of the levee onto the vast heap below, I took a slightly deeper breath and felt my chest swell to fill my imaginary armor.

Ha! Any boy could *play*. Any normal kid could dawdle about, doing nothing of significance. Any underachieving boy could waste time looking for frogs and worms. But *this* boy—this grandson of Willard the Wise—was *working*.

Willard was not in the habit of tossing about compliments by the handfuls. Frugality ran as deep in Willard's expenditures of praise as it ran in his ledger. So, when a word of praise landed on my seven-year-old ear, I seized it, stuffed it inside my imaginary knight's helmet, and tucked it away for later use...when I needed a reminder that I wasn't such a lazy lout after all.

Work, I realized with genuine surprise, *is a gift.*

My grandfather had learned it. My father had learned it. And now they were handing it to me.

My grandfather had learned to appreciate the gift. He knew the priceless value, the incredible sense of significance you obtain by contributing your small part to something much bigger than yourself. He'd developed the ability to imagine what a patch of earth could look like if it were surrounded with a levee made from boulders and cement. Then, after he had envisioned it, he poured himself into it, as a knight pouring himself into battle.

At the end of a day he could see progress toward his vision. At the end of a year, he could see buildings that would house people, bringing not only joy to those who stayed there, but also significance to himself. He must have read and understood Colossians 3:23, which says, "Whatever you do, work at it with all your heart, as working for the Lord, not for men."

Through the years, "Hardcastle Island" served as a popular Oak Creek resort, and my grandfather, recovered from his health problems, began yet another church, this time in the breezeway of The View Motel.

Willard the Builder certainly knew how to turn a detour into a purposeful project. His health-mandated diversion to Sedona, Arizona, brought him to a place where they needed a new church. At the time, he thought his purpose for coming to Oak Creek was to recover from a near-fatal ulcer. But God had another purpose in mind. He needed a church there, and, in His time, Willard the Builder was the man for the job.

As a kid, I wondered what unseen force propelled my grandfather out of bed early every morning and kept him whistling and singing his way through his many projects until after the sun went down again.

Now I know.

Willard the Wise galloped into his projects as a warrior gallops into battle. Why? Because he had learned the secret to work.

He enjoyed it.

Work, for him, was a spiritual quest, almost as much fun as play. Maybe more so. Because he knew that God had created work for a purpose, to serve others and to provide a sense of significance. Work, Willard understood, was God's way of allowing our tiny contribution to His vast kingdom…like my little pile of leaves added to the great and towering pile already begun.

Small though my contribution had been, Willard had noticed and commended me. My grandfather knew that he existed for a greater purpose than simply earning a living for himself and his family. Apart from God's eternal purposes, all his hard work would simply become, as Solomon penned in Ecclesiastes, "a chasing after the wind." Without an eternal purpose to motivate his actions, all the wealth he obtained from his hard work would simply be left for others to use or lose.

Knowing my granddaddy as I did, I'm sure the words of Paul bounced around in his heart, too.

Therefore, my dear brothers, stand firm. Let nothing move you. Always give yourselves fully to the work of the Lord, because you know that your labor in the Lord is not in vain. (1 Corinthians 15:58)

Work, he knew, is a gift from the hand of God. Without His purposes, work is meaningless. But with His purposes, with *Him,* work becomes something transcendent...reaching beyond time into eternity.

And because Willard possessed this wonderful knowledge, his contributions to the kingdom, board by board, nail by nail, were used by the Creator of the universe to help accomplish His purpose...drawing more people into a relationship with Himself.

That's what I learned during an imaginative detour on Hardcastle's Island in Oak Creek Canyon, from a weathered grandfather who was short in stature and long in purpose. *It is the Lord Christ you are serving.*

Every nail driven in His name will be remembered forever. So will every raked leaf. Nothing done for Him and His kingdom is ever wasted. I know that now, and it comforts me.

It is the legacy of Willard the Wise.

CHAPTER THREE

Prepared for the Storm

I picked up a green olive and popped it in my mouth just as my mother caught me in the act.

"I *saw* that, Clark Cothern, and that's enough! Save room for dinner."

I laughed and scampered through my grandmother's kitchen door, down the two nine-inch steps onto the cement driveway and heard a small splash at the same time I felt water seeping into my tennis shoes.

It had been three years since the first time I set foot on the island. Since that time, my grandfather had built eleven cottages on the property, plus his own home, plus a four-unit apartment building. His island resort business was booming.

All the renters had been evacuated hours earlier, since the weather reports had issued a flash flood warning. Unexpected early fall snows were melting from the mountains up the Oak Creek Canyon all the way to Flagstaff. The unusually heavy

November rains were adding to the creek's flood-level volume by the minute.

The scent of our soon-to-be sumptuous Thanksgiving feast beckoned us to stay and ride out the storm. Thanksgiving on Hardcastle's Island was always a five-star event. Grandmother was serious about her holiday cooking. She would never think of using that "store-bought" dressing. And to her way of thinking, to use canned cranberry jelly would be like preaching false doctrine. She and my mother had been dressing the bird and the table with delectable taste. Our mouths had been watering all morning.

Though Granddaddy insisted on evacuating the renters, he was sure we could stay. It looked for a while like Thanksgiving dinner would not be spoiled by a little old flood.

Every half hour, he would walk to the creek bed, look at the water level, and say, "There's nothing to worry about." I could tell my mom was worried, though. Dad would laugh, pat Mom on the shoulder, and say, "Now, dear, we're going to be just fine. Remember, your *father* built this place."

But the strategically placed wrinkles in her forehead broadcast her inner turmoil as she watched the only footbridge off the island being torn apart and carried away like toothpicks by the rising water.

I was becoming increasingly thankful for the levee and for Granddaddy's incredible persistence which had placed it there. Three years earlier I had watched Granddaddy drive to different parts of the canyon where he grunted, groaned, bent, lifted, and loaded boulders into the faded pink pickup until the old rig sagged on its springs.

At the time, I might as well have been one of Noah's skeptical neighbors. In all my seven whole years of being alive, I had never once seen the creek rise high enough to run around the north side of the island. *Geesh,* I thought, *either this guy knows something I don't, or he's just a glutton for punishment.* (I can imagine that building an ark must have been a whopper of a detour from Noah's previous dry-land plans!)

Yet all through those three summers, in the blazing Arizona sun, Willard had placed those boulders—thousands of them, one at a time—against the island's embankment, all around the creek side. He doubled his efforts and the number of boulders near the point where the water would split and run around through the dry creek bed to the north. Then he had cranked up the cement mixer (powered by a lawn mower engine), and, one back-aching bucketful at a time, he had poured cement around the boulders.

If there was one thing Willard possessed plenty of, it was foresight.

If there was another thing Willard had, it was persistence. Three years' worth.

Those two ingredients, blended with some sand, cement mix, and water, resulted in a veritable fortress, poised in readiness against the onslaught of a potential flood…like the one we were now experiencing.

His faithful persistence had built a strong foundation.

I thought about how wise Willard had been to build such a stubborn structure as I watched the water rise in the north creek bed—the one that was usually dry—which by this time was impossible to cross. The fast-flowing stream had long ago washed away the dirt piled over the aluminum culverts, and we were now stuck on the island like turtles on a log.

Where there had been only dirt, there was now water. But where there had been concrete and boulders, there was land. I was starting to catch the drift of the story of the man who built his house on a rock: *A good foundation really does make a difference when the floods hit.*

I remembered the first time I had seen this patch of earth, and my reaction to it. Both my dad and my grandfather had been right. They knew this place really could turn into an island. Now, at age ten, I was beginning to wonder if it would remain an island, or if it would become part of the Oak Creek Canyon Natural Creek Bed Relocation Program.

The levee was holding just fine, but the water was high enough on the north side of the island to creep over into the lower spots, creating the inch of water in the carport, where we tiptoed across to higher ground, awaiting Granddaddy's decision. Would he elect to stay on the island and ride out the storm, or would we be hauled off to safety?

Though my mom looked concerned, I kept my eye on my dad. His spirits didn't seem dampened at all by the rising waters. Of course, he had helped build the levee, so he knew firsthand of its protective strength. He obviously had faith in the foundation, too.

It was after the footbridge washed out that Granddaddy made up his mind. He called a utility company and they said they would send some workmen out to see what they could do.

I snitched two more olives before Grandmother packed away all the taste-tempting morsels into the fridge. Sadly, I watched the feast being plastic-wrapped and put away: turkey, cranberry dressing, stuffing, sweet potatoes, relish tray…it was enough to bring tears to your eyes, not to mention a pang to your stomach.

We all walked over to what used to be the road. On the other side of what now looked like a brown, raging river, the utility truck had arrived. It was a huge boom truck, complete with flashing amber lights, a lift bucket, and a powerful winch with a hundred feet of cable attached to the front bumper. A couple of men shot a cable across the creek. My father and grandfather attached the cable around a huge tree on the edge of the embankment, close to the spot where we had raked leaves into the previously dry creek bed.

The rescuers ran their end around a post on the second-story deck of cottage number eleven and tightened it with the truck's winch. They then hung a large pulley over the cable and suspended a chairlike gizmo from the pulley.

This was getting exciting. Just like in the movies.

A long rope allowed Dad to pull the chair from our side and the utility men to pull from their side, creating an open-air cable car ferry. Man! I wished I had one of those things in my backyard back home in Phoenix.

While the men on the opposite bank kept the rope taut, Dad hauled the chair across to our side of the creek. Then, beginning with my demure little grandmother, they started the island exodus, from the land flowing with milk, honey, dinner rolls, turkey, dressing, and plenty of olives, to the promised terra firma.

Grandmother looked like a petite queen of England sitting on her throne, holding tight to her scarf so as not to disturb her hair—carefully styled for Thanksgiving. The pillowcase in her lap contained a few special family pictures, the only items she thought important enough to take off the island at the last minute. She looked so regal that I half expected her to wave, fingers together, in queenly fashion as she glided across the chasm to the royal balcony on the other side. (Where's a video camera when you need one?)

Next, my mother took her turn, looking a bit more frightened than my grandmother had, but trying to enjoy the ride. Then my sister Kathey took a spin on the chair, with the men on the other side pulling ever so carefully as my father released enough slack from his line to keep the rope from sagging into the strong current.

I couldn't wait for my turn. Even Disneyland couldn't compete with this ride. As I climbed up into the chair I thought, *This has got to be the neatest Thanksgiving trip we've ever taken!*

Granddaddy steadied the chair while Dad tied a belt around my waist, just in case the chair tipped or jerked. Over the roar of the creek, he hollered, "Hold on tight!" I didn't need a reminder. I was already leaving my fingerprints deep in the steel supports. I grinned from ear to ear and removed one hand briefly enough to give a military salute to my father, who smiled and saluted back.

I gaped at the raging water less than three feet below my feet and dropped my jaw as boulders the size of my dad's desk tumbled downstream like marbles. Entire sixty-foot-long sycamore trees, uprooted by the torrent, shot through the canyon as though rocket-propelled.

I had heard about the great worldwide flood in Sunday school, the one where Noah and his family escaped the total destruction of the earth's surface. In that moment, I began to understand a little better how those poor people who failed to heed God's warnings must have felt as they watched the waters rise.

Just before the rescuers arrived, my dad had joked to my mother, "Now, dear, you know that God promised never again to destroy the whole earth with a flood. That's why He gave us a rainbow—as a promise, remember?"

"Yes," she retorted, "but He didn't say anything about wiping out a little island in a canyon."

We all watched from the other side of the creek as Granddaddy, the last one off the island, tied himself in the chair, untied the rope from his end, dropping it near the tree, and began his trek across the creek. One of the utility workers slapped me on the back and asked, "We need to get our cable back. Do you want to swim across and untie it for us?"

I raised my eyebrows, smiled, and shook my head no. Everyone laughed. He said, "We'll be back in a day or two to get it...*after* the water level goes down a bit." We thanked them and headed, in my dad's car—which he'd left parked on the other side of the creek—up the hill toward town.

We all spent the night in a motel by the highway. Our Thanksgiving "feast" consisted of ham sandwiches and store-bought potato salad. Even though we were seated on motel room beds instead of around Grandmother's festively trimmed table, Dad led the thanksgiving prayer.

"Lord, we are truly thankful," he said, "not only for this food, which is going to taste *really* good after a day like today, but also for our very lives, which we realize are a gift from You. Thank You for keeping us all safe, warm, and dry. We have much to be thankful for. Amen."

At the crack of dawn the very next day, Willard began surveying the island property, looking for a way to build a bridge that wouldn't wash out the next time it flooded. With the exception of the bridges, however, the island had remained intact. A few low spots still revealed a puddle or two, but the island had survived. Not a single building had been lost or even damaged by the floodwaters.

Granddaddy's faithful persistence paid off. The levee held.

The following June, when we next visited Oak Creek, Granddaddy displayed his new bridge. "Go ahead, drive over it," he said proudly. "It will handle any automobile you can drive over it." I believed him. The deck was made of railroad ties.

Thirty years later, my wife and I and my mother visited the island, now owned by someone else. I'm proud to proclaim that the island is still there, now named Newcastle Island, and Granddaddy's bridge is still standing. Under the cool shade of those massive creekside trees, we shared some ham sandwiches in memory of our adventurous island rescue. With our souls being restored beside the still waters, we recalled a few of our family's detours.

My mother, still seizing "teachable moments" with her kids after all these years, asked, "You know what your grand-father taught me through that flood?" I leaned back against a large rock and braced myself for the life lesson she was about to offer. "What's that, Mom?"

"It seems to me that his persistence building that levee paid off. But you know, it wasn't just faith in his hard work that saved the island."

I swallowed the last bite of my sandwich and waited for her explanation. "Oh?"

"Your grandfather didn't place his trust in the boulders and cement he put there around the island. He put his faith in

God. But he didn't have the kind of blind faith that expected God to keep natural disasters from happening. He put his faith into *action* and put in a lot of hard work to prepare for the storms."

I nodded and took a sip of iced tea. I could tell by her wistful look that she wasn't quite finished, so I kept quiet and waited for the rest of her message about faith and strong foundations.

"It seems to me that when we place our faith in the solid Rock—Jesus Christ—He still expects us to *do* something with that faith. Sometimes it's hard work to step out in faith when we know we've got a difficult job to do, but that persistent effort builds a strong foundation. Every time we step out in faith and do what's right, even though it's hard work it makes the foundation a little stronger. Then when the storms hit, the foundation keeps you from getting washed away."

I watched the placid waters of Oak Creek trickling by and thought about what a huge difference those rains had made in the canyon's demeanor.

"You're right, Mom," I said, crunching a potato chip. "That would make a good chapter for a book some day." (Little did she know...)

When we had finished our drive back down to Phoenix to my parents' house that night, I looked up Matthew 7:24–27 and realized just how right she was. Jesus Himself, talking about a guy who built a house, said, "Everyone who hears these words of mine [about living out your faith so others can see evidence of it] and puts them into practice is like a wise man who built his house on the rock. The rain came down, the streams rose, and the winds blew and beat against that house; yet it did not fall, because it had its foundation on the rock."

For Willard, storms—and even floods—became calls to action. He was prepared for the storms, literally, emotionally, and spiritually, because he not only heard Jesus' words, but he acted on them. He "put them into practice." And because of his faith in action, Willard possessed the amazing ability to see God's handiwork smack-dab in the middle of a disaster. The reason he wasn't too anxious when the storms hit was because he had built a solid foundation, one boulder at a time.

My detour from a sumptuous Thanksgiving dinner on Hardcastle's Island to a ham sandwich in a Sedona motel revealed to me that sometimes it takes a flood to show me the condition of my foundation. And it affirmed in me that the persistent, hard work of faith-building will keep me steady through the storm, because my faith is built on the solid Rock Himself.

CHAPTER FOUR

Mickey Leads the Way

"Oh NO!"

I could hear Mom's voice through the vent in the bathroom. All I heard were those two words—and the kind of groan you make when words are useless.

It was 10:15 P.M., a full forty-five minutes past my bedtime. But like any sleep-resistant ten-year-old, I had dawdled and was just then brushing my teeth. Finishing up quickly, I crept down the hall and around the corner to see if I could figure out what was happening.

"Yes," Mom was saying, "we'll load up right away and take turns driving. We should be able to make it by around noon tomorrow."

Wow. This must be serious. She was obviously talking about an all-night trip. But to where? And why? I had school tomorrow. Was I going to be left with a baby-sitter?

"Okay, thanks, Ricci, we'll see you very soon."

Ah. Aunt Ricci. That was an important clue. It had to be someone on Dad's side of the family, in New Mexico. Ricci was Dad's youngest sister and a cool aunt by anyone's standards. She loved to tease, to laugh, and even drove us to the root beer place.

"Oh, and Ricci? Tell Jeannie we love her and we're praying for her. Okay. Bye."

Jeannie was another of Dad's sisters. Something had happened to someone in Aunt Jeannie's family. It was just like Aunt Ricci to become news bearer to the rest of the family. A dispatcher at the state police office in Tucumcari, she did "messages" for a living. Even the tough ones.

Mom hung up the phone, and I took a hesitant step into the study where she was standing, eyes closed, shaking her head and taking deep breaths.

I figured I wouldn't get in trouble for staying up too late, seeing that she was preoccupied with matters far more important than my bedtime. So I took another step into the room, where I knew she would see me the next time she opened her eyes.

Looking up, Mom sat down on her swivel chair, motioned me over, and pulled me up onto her lap. She held me close and rocked me, even though I was well past the age when she normally did the rocking thing. I figured it was as much for her benefit as mine. She was obviously preparing me for the bad news she'd just received.

I didn't have to ask for information, since I knew she was working up to telling me. She took her time, probably wording it carefully in her mind before it came out of her mouth.

"You know your cousin Mickey, in New Mexico?"

Thoughts formed as quickly as shots fired and began ricocheting around in my brain. Of course I knew Mickey. He was the older cowboy cousin who taught me how to jump off a horse into a pile of hay. He was the athletic cousin who could smack a baseball clean over the center field fence. He was the courageous cousin who had led his brother, my sister, and me out of the Grand Canyon to get help when my father had grown faint from heat exhaustion.

Yeah, I knew Mickey. He was cool.

But what about him? I knew I was about to get the answer, so I just waited while Mom sighed again, rocked me some more, and carefully crafted her sentence.

"Well..." She adjusted me on her knee, then took one more deep breath, drawing in strength along with the air. "Mickey was swimming across a small lake with his Boy Scout troop, and when some of the boys looked back to see where he was, they—didn't see him. Anywhere."

I wrinkled my forehead. This wasn't sounding good. I was pretty sure where the conversation was headed, but I didn't want it to go there.

"They swam back to see if he was playing a trick on them by hiding under the water for a few seconds, but...he..."

Her voice was really strained, and it seemed to stop, as if something just closed off the air. She swallowed and tried to finish.

"He...just wasn't there."

She paused again, shaking her head. It was almost as though she was telling the story in order to convince herself that what she'd just heard on the phone had really happened.

"They had to send some divers to look for him. They

39

found his body a couple of hours later."

So that was the news. Mickey was dead. She rocked me some more as we both tried to let her words sink in.

"He's gone. I just can't believe it. Aunt Jeannie must be beside herself."

My cousin, the guy I looked up to and played with every time we traveled to New Mexico for Christmas vacation, had drowned. He would never be alive on earth again. Never. No more horse rides. No more hiking. No more baseball.

But it *couldn't* be. Mickey was young, healthy, active.... I knew in my mind what my mother had just told me was true, and I knew she wouldn't lie, but my heart didn't want to hold on to what my mind had just heard.

He was really gone.

I found myself swimming across a lake, along with a bunch of Boy Scouts. I looked behind me and saw nothing but water. In a panic, I dove underwater and began searching furiously. For Mickey. But all I could see was greenish murky water and seaweed. My lungs were about to burst, but I couldn't come up for air. I had to find him. I just had to...

Just then I woke up, gasping a huge, deep breath, as though I hadn't taken in oxygen for a whole minute. My entire bed vibrated, as though in constant motion. A humming noise droned beneath my room. It was terribly dark, but I saw a few specks of light, and, as my head cleared, realized they were stars.

What were stars doing in my room? But wait, my room was moving. Quickly. And what was that noise?

As I rubbed my eyes and looked around, it dawned on me where I was. I was stretched out in the very back of my parents' '59 Chevy station wagon, on a makeshift bed atop suitcases and a sleeping bag.

The stars shone brightly through the back window, since we were in the desert and no city lights muted their brilliance. The drone turned out to be the sound of four tires spinning against the highway—a sound punctuated by the occasional whoosh of a car or truck passing in the opposite lane.

Oh yeah, I remembered, with a sick feeling in the pit of my stomach. *He's gone.*

"Dead." I mouthed the word without actually pushing any air through my vocal chords. I wondered what it was like to feel dead. I had never had to say that word about any of my close relatives before. It was strange to describe someone you actually *knew* with that term.

I remembered why we were traveling all night. I was about to attend the funeral of the cousin who had been so vibrant and alive just a day earlier. And now he was gone, forever. Well, maybe not forever. But at least as long as it takes for the rest of us who know Jesus to get to heaven.

I wonder what it will be like, I thought. *Heaven. I wonder how it felt the moment Mickey quit being alive here and started being alive there. What about the funeral? What will that be like? Will a bunch of people be crying? How will I feel? How am I supposed to feel?*

Those thoughts swam in my head as the tires droned on, carrying our car past the billboard that said "Tucumcari Tonight." I watched the stars, wondering how it would feel to drown, trying to picture the scene at the lake, trying to imagine what it might have been like to be breathing one minute, under water the next, and in heaven the next.

"I can't believe Mickey's dead," I said, so softly that nobody else in the car heard me. I just needed to say it, even if nobody else heard.

The stars became blurry as my eyelids became heavy.

Everything smelled like flowers, as if an entire garden had been moved indoors. I noticed two separate floodlights, one pink and one blue, recessed in the ceiling just above the casket, giving Mickey's face the sort of glow you'd expect to see in a color photograph taken for his senior picture.

The room was air-conditioned, and it felt good to stay inside, even though it meant being in the same room where adults were hugging each other, sniffling, dabbing their eyes with tissues, and talking in hushed tones, as though Mickey would somehow overhear them.

It had only been a few hours since we arrived in Tucumcari, New Mexico—a long, narrow town stretched along the highway leading beyond Albuquerque and on toward Amarillo. Several gas stations, motels, and restaurants lined the strip city, and for eight or ten blocks on either side of the main drag were houses. My grandparents, my father's mom and dad, lived in one of those houses.

I'd been awake since the sun flooded in through the car window, robbing my little space of its comfortable darkness. We had all taken showers at my grandparents' house. For me, Mom had packed a pair of black slacks, a short-sleeved white shirt, and an honest-to-goodness tie that Dad had to knot for me. *This must be an important event,* I thought, *for her to pack the heavy artillery.* Fortunately, even though she'd brought it along in a hanging bag, she didn't make me wear the coat. On top of everything else, I had no desire to swelter.

I stayed toward the back, watching other people mill around, walking in small groups up to the front, standing close to the casket, staring down at Mickey's young face, not saying anything. Some would reach tentatively out and touch his hand. I couldn't figure why they did that. It wasn't creepy or anything like that, but it just didn't seem like the thing you ought to do. I figured maybe it was their way of checking to make sure he was really dead, that he wasn't going to suddenly react to their touch, open his eyes, reach out his fingers and grab their hand and say, "Gotcha!"

It would have been something Mickey would have done.

All the way to the funeral home I'd felt that people must be looking at us, that somehow they must all know that the young man in the real tie was going to his cousin's funeral. When we stopped off at the drugstore to buy some aspirin, I felt almost compelled to tell the lady behind the counter, "The reason I'm dressed up like this is because we're going to a funeral. My cousin. Mickey. He drowned." But I didn't.

I wanted people to somehow know how life-changing this whole thing was. I wished they would ask me what was going on inside my young mind, because I was all prepared with a speech about living life to the fullest since you never knew which breath might be your last, about knowing Christ before your number came up.

But nobody asked. And I kept my speech to myself.

The family was all there, dressed in black. Terry, looking

at his older brother. Aunt Jeannie watching her son, lying in that cold casket. I realized at that moment that there were other people there who were far more deeply affected by Mickey's passing than I was.

The organ stopped playing "Nearer My God to Thee," and my father stood behind a podium and read the obituary notice from the newspaper. I remember thinking how sad his voice sounded. Usually calm and controlled, his voice sounded strange and shaky, and I started silently rooting for him, praying he would make it through without breaking down.

The pastor of Mickey's church stood up and began reading from Scripture. "I tell you a mystery," he read. "We will not all sleep...."

Mickey looks like he's just asleep. He looks like he could wake up and jump right outta there at any second. Like he could throw his legs over the edge, grab his baseball glove, jog down the street to the baseball field, and start hitting grounders.

"But we will all be changed—in a flash, in the twinkling of an eye...."

Mickey was changed, all right. I bet that's how it happened. As soon as his body stopped breathing, I'll bet the change from life to death happened in a flash.

"When the perishable has been clothed with the imperishable, and the mortal with immortality, then the saying that is written will come true: 'Death has been swallowed up in victory.'"

Yeah, victory. I bet he's high-fivin' people up there right now. "Hey, Peter, how's it goin'?" Slap. "Man, I wish I could have taken some lessons from you about walkin' on water, ya know? Oh wow, Moses!" Slap. *"It's good to meet you, sir. I've been meaning to ask you about that Red Sea thing. And Noah!"* Slap. *"I am so glad you're here, too. Listen, how did the door shut on the ark? I mean, did the rising water lift it right up, or did God reach down and just slam it in place?"*

Lost in my own thoughts prompted by the Scripture reading, I don't remember too much of what the pastor said. I do remember, though, that he told a story about when Mickey had accepted Christ as his Savior. That part grabbed my attention, because I'd done that, too. And that, according to what my parents said, and what the pastor read from the Bible, is what would allow Mickey to get into heaven.

The pastor said, "Mickey realized that he couldn't get into heaven by doing good deeds…"

He'd done lots of good deeds. He was a Boy Scout, after all. But he knew he couldn't work his way into heaven.

"And he knew that the only way to heaven was through Jesus Christ, the One who said, 'I am the way, the truth and the life. No one comes to the Father except through me.…'"

Is it weird to feel happy at a funeral? I'm sorry Mickey's gone, but this is really great. I'm going to see him again. I've accepted Christ, too. We'll be together again—like it used to be, only better.

Then the pastor told another story. I listened to this one, too. He said, "Once a man was driving with his son in his pickup truck along a dirt road next to a field."

I could picture what he was talking about. It was right out of a Tucumcari afternoon. I had ridden in pickup trucks, too, sometimes with my dad at the wheel.

He continued, "A bee flew in the window and the little boy

began yelling, 'Get it away, get it away!' It seems the boy was allergic to bee stings. A single sting could be fatal."

Wow. Must have been scary.

"The dad reached up to the windshield and trapped the bee inside his hand. Then he held out his fist, turned his fingers upward, and let the bee go. It started flying around inside the cab of the truck again."

Oh, man. Why didn't he kill it? I was really into this story.

"The boy started screaming again, but the dad held out his palm and said, 'Son, it's okay. See the stinger there? I took the sting for you. You don't have to worry anymore.'"

Even at ten years old I got the pastor's point. Even though we were scared and sad because of Mickey's death, we didn't have to fear death anymore, because Jesus conquered sin and death once and for all. He took the sting.

Now the verse he had read made sense.

Where, O death, is your victory?
Where, O death, is your sting?

I thought about that story as they closed the casket lid and my Aunt Jeannie cried a little. That was the hardest part of the funeral for me. When the casket lid was shut. Probably because I knew I would never see Mickey's face again, at least not on earth. But that story about the dad and his son and the bee helped.

I thought about it as we drove in a long line of cars to the cemetery. I thought about it as the Little League ball players lined up at the chain-link fence as we passed. They all took off their hats and held them over their hearts, in honor of my cousin Mickey.

And I thought about it as we drove all the way home to Phoenix the next day. The detour, from brushing my teeth and crawling into bed to an all-night drive to the funeral of my cousin, cemented for me the fact that the human mortality rate is indeed 100 percent. We are, as the pastor had said, all destined to die, and after that, to face the judgment. But for those who know Christ, funerals are really commencement exercises. For those who know Christ, our grief is temporary. Our future is filled with the promise of a reunion.

That detour changed me.

Oh, sure, I'd known all about those Scripture passages. (I was a preacher's kid, after all.) I'd even been to funerals before. But those were for *other* people's cousins. Not mine. This one was different. This was Mickey.

Before, funerals had been like watching other people ride a roller coaster. I saw them get frightened before they got on the ride, scream their lungs out while on the ride, and then smile and laugh about what a great ride it was after they finished the ride. But this time, this funeral, was like experiencing the ride for myself.

I moved the reality of death from the shelf in my young brain marked "fact" to the one labeled "conviction." Now I knew personally what great news it was that Christ paid my debt of sin. It wasn't for some "pie in the sky by and by" (whatever that meant). It was so I could see Mickey and other loved ones again. It was so I didn't have to fear death. I knew now, without a doubt, that the next time I saw my cousin, it would be face to face. The same way it would be when I finally got to meet Christ.

Oh, sure, I figured the ride would still be scary, but when

the ride stops and I step off, it won't be frightening at all. It will be thrilling. Now I can look forward to a joyful reunion, with my loved ones, and with Jesus.

Because He's the One who took the ultimate fear out of death. He took the sting for me.

Now I'm looking forward to heaven. Because right after I get introduced to Jesus, I'm going to ask Him to show me where Mickey lives. But knowing Mickey, he'll probably be standing there with a big grin on his face the moment I walk in the door.

"Clark," he'll say, "what in the world *took* you so long?"

CHAPTER FIVE

The Shepherd of Arlington

I watched a scrawny jackrabbit leap from behind a clump of sagebrush and bound across the dry riverbed. Was something after it?

My dad spoke suddenly, shattering fifteen minutes of silence in the car following the morning service.

"They want me to come back again tonight and preach the evening service."

I lost sight of the rabbit, sighed, and gazed across the expanse of desolation stretching out to the hazy horizon. There hadn't been much to talk about on the long drive back to Phoenix. At least two of us in the car had been thinking, "I'm glad *that's* over."

We had just crossed the tiny bridge over the slithering stretch of sand they called a riverbed, rounding the corner by the tiny gas-station-turned-convenience-mart that passed for a town called Hassyampa.

Registering what my dad had just said, my sister and I shot each other a look, each knowing what the other was thinking. *Oh no. He's not serious…is he?*

"And…" Dad continued, reading our expressions in his rearview mirror, "I told them we would."

We. He used the word WE.

Just after Dad said that, I suddenly felt my insides go *whoops.* It was partly because of the announcement, and partly because the car flew at sixty miles per hour over a rise in the road, followed by a hefty dip on the other side. It was the roller-coaster-like plunge that threatens to turn your innards into outards. Earlier that day, the first time we sped through that Hassyampa dip, my dad had been pointing out all the interesting sights as he drove me, my sister, and my mother to the little white church on the hill in Arlington, Arizona.

If there were any "interesting sights" in Arlington, I couldn't name one. All I saw was a tiny general store with a single gas pump in front, a post office the size of a postage stamp, and a couple of stray dogs.

That single building. That was it. The town.

"The thriving metropolis of Arlington, Arizona," my dad had said, and with such enthusiasm you'd have thought we were doing Mount Rushmore. This deserted place looked more like Mount St. Helens, *after* the eruption.

I noticed Dad had used the term *town* loosely as he'd said, "The church is actually about a mile past town." *If this is the town, then what's the church gonna look like?* I wondered.

Dad had helped start and grow several small churches, all within driving distance of our home in Phoenix. That meant— unlike most other preacher's kids I knew—I'd been able to live in the same house through all of my growing-up years.

My limited experience with other "PKs" had taught me they were a lot like military brats. Must have had something to do with trying to prove to the other kids that preachers' kids are human, too. Or maybe it was because they were angry at their parents, or at their former churches, or at God, for moving them around so often. I knew not all preachers' kids were angry and rebellious, but the few I had met could win cussing contests.

My situation was different, and I knew it. My folks didn't really treat my sister and me like preacher's kids, even though we were. Compared with some of the kids I knew, whose parents kept them on a tight leash, my parents had given me plenty of slack, allowing lots of room for mistakes. They figured I'd learn more from my mistakes (which I did), than I would from my successes, as long as they let me suffer the consequences of my own actions (which they did).

A lot of the ministers' kids I knew fell into one of two categories: either they got bailed out a lot by their folks, as though their parents had to "make it okay" when their kids messed up, or the kids got told how to act in every situation. Either way, it seemed the kids just naturally felt the need to rebel.

Dad worked a nine-to-five job as an engineer and then spent evenings and weekends helping these little churches located in or around the Valley of the Sun. At the time I didn't think it was so extraordinary, considering how many other dads did "other stuff" during their evenings and weekends.

Kent's daddy next door built cabinets in his spare time. Bobby's dad across the street made model airplanes that flew by remote control. It just happened that my dad spent his extra time building churches. No big deal.

But today marked a major change in my childhood plan of action. Today we had taken one small step into the desert west of Phoenix, and one giant leap away from a church located only a mile from our house—a really fun church on Thomas Road near 59th Avenue. I could remember all twelve of us sitting in the little sanctuary, watching a tiny black-and-white television as Neil Armstrong stepped onto the moon. That had been a really cool, history-making Wednesday-night prayer meeting. You could do stuff like that when you were in little churches.

I remember some of the adults saying a little prayer after that big event. Something like, "Thank You, Lord, for giving these men a safe journey"—as if they'd just arrived at Aunt Margie's house for Thanksgiving. I guess the prayer for the astronauts transformed the TV event into "official church business," so it was okay to watch it. But just that once. I never did convince my parents there was any spiritual value in my watching *Mission Impossible* on other prayer meeting nights when I was the only kid who showed up.

But Wednesday-night television vanished like a mirage as I looked through the heat waves at the wasteland around me, with its mesquite bushes and cacti and its tiny little village called Arlington.

What kind of people would actually choose to live in a place like this? I consoled myself with the assurance that Dad was only doing pulpit supply; that is, only filling in to preach just this once. I'd traveled with him before on these temporary missions, to little outposts that weren't even on the map.

My favorite times were when he flew to his preaching gigs,

piloted by volunteers in an organization called Wings for Christ. The thought of buzzing over the cacti and lava-strewn hills of southeastern Arizona and into New Mexico made it a little easier to get up at 4:30 A.M. on a Sunday morning. We landed on dirt runways carved out of farmers' fields behind little wooden churches with corrugated aluminum roofs.

And after the morning services, during the potluck lunches served in hot cinder-block fellowship halls with cool concrete floors, we ate every conceivable type of fruit baptized in Jell-O. I could have easily done without some of the lunches, but the cold spaghetti and warm Jell-O were worth the flights back to Phoenix. My dad got to sit in the copilot's seat, to the right of the pilot, and I sat behind both of them in the tiny jump seat. I figured my dad would probably have crossed crocodile-infested waters in a canoe if he thought there was a little church with no preacher to bring the Good News.

So, with visions of rattlesnakes and Gila monsters wriggling under metal folding chairs in a tiny auditorium, I steadied myself with the same thought I'd used every other time when I knew Dad was going to "supply."

It's only for one day.

That was my mantra on this trip to the thriving metropolis of Arlington. I clicked my black church shoes' heels together and thought: *It's only for one day. It's only for one day.*

We drove up the hill onto a barren dirt parking lot and looked at the dilapidated white building with a wooden bell tower atop the tiny porch entrance and restrooms in a little add-on structure around back. The bathrooms were important to me, since it was a full hour's drive from our house in Phoenix to this little dump called Arlington. My urgency to get to the washroom was matched only by my desire to get out of that car. My sister had been droning on and on about her latest boyfriend and I'd had all I could take. She was at *that* age.

Wondering what wild animals had used the facilities before I had, I looked around at this rust-stained outhouse they called a restroom, ventilated with two cowboy boot-sized holes near the bottom of the door. I was afraid to touch anything, wishing I was back in the city where civilized people enjoyed indoor plumbing. When I went to wash up, I turned the right handle on the sink faucet.

Nothing happened.

Oh great. No water in this dust bowl.

Then I tried the handle on the left.

A faint groan issued from subterranean depths, followed by a gurgle, then silence. Suddenly the plumbing coughed twice, made a spooky strangling sound, then with a great spurt shot a massive belch of air, and yellowish brown water shot from the spigot into the sink, ricocheting out onto my trousers. Right where boys in the seventh grade hate to get wet. I was at *that* age.

Evidently, some directionally dyslexic volunteer plumber had connected the cold water pipe to the hot water valve. But of course. Why not? Out here in this forsaken place, why would it be important to connect the hot water side at all? Why would scorpions and coyotes need hot water?

Hardly anything green grew anywhere out here, except under the bathroom sink, where a leak in the only working pipe had given hope to a hearty desert weed of some sort. Outside again, I peered over the rise, spying what I thought were the tops of what looked like trees, although they could have been a mirage. Wavy heat lines blurred my vision over the horizon…and it was only nine in the morning.

Of course there were no paper towels, so with my air-dried hands I brushed as much of the rusty water off my pants as I could and wandered over to our car, the only evidence of human life in sight. Surveying this desolate outpost, I noticed the propane tank that sat sideways between the parking area and the church like a giant, hot-dog-shaped hitching post. I wouldn't have been surprised if Clint Eastwood had ridden up, spat tobacco on a lizard's head, and then sauntered off into the morning sun.

My only consolation was the fact that this torture would be temporary.

Or so I thought.

My dad wouldn't spring his little surprise on us until four hours later.

We. He used the word WE. Here we were, losing our stomachs on the rises and dips near that ghost town of a place called Hassyampa, and my dad was telling us that *we* were going to endure this roller-coaster ride to the wilderness again for the evening service.

We were all going to suffer another hour-long drive in the car, another hour-long service in that building, another disgusting trip to that shack they called a bathroom, and another hour-long drive back home.

It certainly wasn't my idea of a day of rest.

Sunday evenings had to this point been something of a pleasant prospect. I could ride my bike to our city church and sit with my friends. After the service, several of us would hop the fence and play on the swings at the school playground next door.

But now an irresistible outside force, my father, had swept in and changed everything. With the lawns and trees and amiable relationships of civilization far behind, he had led me away from the city to wander in the desert. Dad might as well have been Moses, and I might as well have been a grumbling Israelite, longing for the tastes of home.

In other words, I'd been detoured. The highway our family traveled that Sunday was not the road I wanted to be traveling at all.

But, strangely enough, looking back at that road filled with rises and dips, I can see how God was preparing to teach me an unforgettable life lesson. I didn't know it at the time, but God was getting ready to show me: *You can't tell a book by its cover, and you can't judge the worth of a saint by his or her outward appearance.*

He taught me that lesson through Gussy Estes. Gussy's skin was as wrinkled as beef jerky. This sun-leathered, desert-dwelling grandma would never be a candidate for the cover of a ladies' magazine, but inside Gussy—where the spirit dwells— was the stuff of which saints are made.

The way Gussy greeted us, you'd have thought we were her long-lost relatives, returning home from our voyage on the *Titanic*. Her warm, accepting, crinkly smile, complete with several missing teeth, was enough to make you forget all about the rust stains on your pants.

Gussy and her husband, Charlie, we later discovered, had donated the land for the church building. She lived in a little two-bedroom trailer over the rise where I'd seen the trees.

Then there were the three Johns.

First John was named John Riddle, a retired railroad man who'd probably seen more steam engines than diesel. First John and his tiny wife, Louise (who had diabetes and had to drink orange juice toward the end of Sunday school), couldn't wait for us to come back again on another Sunday. They wanted to invite us to dinner so we could enjoy John's famous "cat heads" (his odd name for biscuits) and gravy.

I thought I'd be spared the cat head experience since this would obviously be the only Sunday we would make our appearance.

Second John's last name (we learned from First John) was Cassady, a muscular former Navy man half the age of First John. Mr. Cassady had one glass eye—and a keen one at that. With his good eye sighting down a pellet rifle he could pick off a bird sitting atop a telephone pole fifty feet away. John and his wife, Pat, liked to barbecue, because John, a butcher by trade, knew how to pick the prime cuts.

Third John's real first name was Juan. Juan Arviso, a large, happy Mexican man whose wife, Lilly, could make homemade tortillas that melted in your mouth like snowflakes.

Meeting these nice people made coming back for the evening service a little more bearable. But as shocked as we were the first time Dad said we would return, we were even more shocked when he said, "We (he used the term "we" a lot) would be happy to come back next week."

Then on the second Sunday, they asked him to consider coming again for one more Sunday. Again, he said "we" would.

After the third trip to Arlington, Gussy invited us over for dinner at her trailer. I'd heard my mom call Gussy a "diamond in the rough," and during that afternoon we spent with her, I began to catch a glint of the shiny stuff inside a weather-beaten body—something my parents had seen right away. Yeah, there were the piles of clothes in the corner (not the way my mom kept house), and there were the four geese that nipped at my heels when I walked across her junk-strewn lawn, but still and all, Gussy was quite a lady.

I think the shiny stuff many people might have missed was the light of Jesus. Compared with some of our city friends, Gussy didn't have much, but what she did have, she gave away with an open hand and a smile. And she had that way of making us feel that we had done *her* a favor, since by receiving her gift, we had brought her such joy.

After the evening service the night of that third trip, a delegation consisting of Gussy and the First and Second Johns caught my dad outside by the propane tank. Second John cleared his throat, looked into my dad's eyes with his one good eye, and said, "Gaylon, we just took a vote, and it's unanimous. We just called you to be our pastor."

During the car trip back to Phoenix, Dad told us what they had said, and we all chuckled. How sweet. They certainly weren't steeped in formality, but it was a kind gesture to tell Dad they wanted him to be their pastor.

Of course we expected him to say what he'd said before in other situations: "Well, thanks for the vote of confidence, but I'm not available to serve as your full-time pastor. I'd be happy to fill in while you look for someone else, though."

After three Sundays (I had to admit) the people were kind

of growing on us. But I would have been shocked—stunned—to hear Dad say, "I accept."

But that's just what he did.

He waited until we got to Hassyampa again to break the news. (I was beginning to dread the dips near Hassyampa.)

My sister blurted out, "You're kidding!"

I whined, "I don't believe it!"

That was one of only a few times in all my growing-up years when I saw my dad get visibly upset. His ears turned righteous-indignation red, his chest puffed up, and his shoulders straightened. With more passion in his voice than I had heard in a long time, he said, "These people deserve a shepherd, too."

When the rest of his sermon came rolling off his tongue in one, long stream, I got the impression he'd been rehearsing since we pulled away from the church parking lot.

"It may be a small church, and they might not have the largest youth group or the greatest programs, but these people love the Lord, and they want someone to teach them, to lead them, and...well, *love* them. And they called *me* to be that someone."

He breathed hard for a moment, and then brought the message to a close.

"And I've accepted."

End of speech.

That was that.

We sat sullenly, accepting the sentence we'd just been handed by the judge. Mentally, I began to prepare myself for *years* of misery, wandering in this scorching, snake-infested patch of dirt they called Arlington.

But as it turned out, it wasn't misery at all.

Over the next six years, I ate often at Gussy's table, sampled dozens of John Riddle's cat heads (with gravy), dined on delectable barbecue from select steaks at the Cassadys, and ate my weight in Lilly Arviso's tasty, paper-thin tortillas.

We worshiped together. Laughed together. Wept together. Grew together. And somehow the six years didn't seem so very long after all.

The detour from a comfortable city church down the dusty desert road through Arlington took me directly into the hearts of these saints, whose lives were seasoned with salt and light. Strangely enough, with all the stomach-flipping rises and dips near Hassyampa, one of the biggest occurred on my last trip back to Phoenix, before moving away to attend college.

Speeding away from Arlington, I felt suddenly empty. Homesick. Like you do when you leave family.

I looked at the high school graduation cards and gifts piled on the seat next to me and felt a certain pride. These good people were sending me off to the big city university as though I was their fair-haired boy going off to war.

Dad stayed on as their pastor for two more years after I left for college. My parents wore out two cars in the eight years they served that little congregation. And dear, sweet, wrinkled old Gussy remained one of our family's most loyal friends, even after Dad took another assignment helping start another church.

Years later, when Dad heard that Gussy was in the hospital in Phoenix, he drove over to see her. He prayed with her and reminded her that someone saw the saint inside.

She squeezed his hand tightly and rasped, "Gaylon, you

always was my pastor, and always will be. I love you and your family like you was my own kin."

Dad, choking back the tears, said, "We love you too, Gussy. We love you too."

Gussy died a few weeks later, and guess who performed the funeral?

Yep, the man who had said, with great passion, "These people deserve a shepherd too."

Arlington, and the people we met there, were not what you would have called glamorous. Ah, but outward appearances can be deceiving, can't they? The generous hearts of those gracious desert-dwelling saints outshone most of the city slickers I had met up to that point in my youthful pilgrimage.

You can't tell a book by its cover, or a town by its looks. And you sure can't tell a saint by his or her skin. You have to look down deeper, where the soul lives, to see the real diamond inside that lump of coal.

It's amazing how things look when you first see them...and how different they appear once you recognize the purpose for which you were brought there. Sometimes it takes a long second look at situations—and people—before you see the touch of God.

I learned about that second look on a long detour through a place called Arlington, Arizona.

CHAPTER SIX

Water Heater Moments

*S*plash.

"Oh, my goodness."

My dad took one more step inside the front door. Hearing another splash, he said again, only slower, and with even more tension in his voice, "Ohhh, my gooooodness."

Following him into the living room of our Phoenix house, our feet felt the cause of his broken-record behavior.

First my mother, then my sister, then me. We each stepped in, and as though reading from the same cue card, we each said, in succession, "Oh—my—goodness."

It felt as if we were back in Oak Creek Canyon. *In* the creek.

Dad flipped the light switch and suddenly, my sleepy eyes popped wide open. The warm, comfortable thoughts of turning in for the night vanished like a good dream when the alarm clock goes off.

A half-inch of water stood where there used to be a floor. In the living room. In the hall. Everywhere.

If we had lived in Alaska, we could have turned the house into a hockey rink. But this was Phoenix. A little too warm for hockey.

We had just driven an hour from Arlington. It had been a typical marathon Sunday: Up early, drive to church, set up, light the gas heaters, help with Sunday school, over to a member's house for lunch, visiting folks all over the countryside all afternoon, back to church for the evening service. Then, on our way home, we stopped at the Mattinglys' who owned the Hassyampa convenience market. They had fed us dinner, which consisted of ham-and-cheese refrigerated sandwiches in cellophane wrappers, warmed in the microwave.

It was nearly eleven and all of us were whipped.

All I wanted to do was crawl in bed. In fact, if I'd been smaller, I probably would have asked for someone to carry me there. But this unusual turn of events was about to rain on our parade—and on our bedtime. To be accurate, it even soaked the dust ruffles on our beds.

We had just been detoured from a typical Sunday night road, which normally dead-ends into a good night's sleep, down Soggy Street into a waterlogged house.

It took a minute for Dad to figure out where the water was coming from. He stood there, scratching his head, and repeating the phrase, "Oh, my goodness," and then suddenly he put his finger up to his lips and said, "Shh. Listen."

We all stood there feeling the water soak into our socks, like a family of bird dogs trying to catch the scent of a pheasant. Noses in the air, heads swiveling back and forth, as though we would hear better at different angles.

Then we heard it. The sound of water running.

It sounded as if someone had brought in the garden hose and turned it on ever so slightly. It just ran, like a steady small stream, into the ocean of floor.

Like a super sleuth with supersonic hearing, Dad followed the sound through the living room and into the hall, where he stopped. We all followed, tiptoeing our way across the living room, where a couple of magazines floated by the coffee table. Halfway down the hall, Dad held up his hand like a platoon leader stopping his men on the trail behind him. I paused with one foot out of the water, frozen like a flamingo. Then he turned his head toward the hall closet.

"There!" he shouted triumphantly. And he whipped open the door.

I don't know what he expected to find there. Perhaps an evil neighbor, sabotaging our house by holding the garden hose in the hall closet?

There was no neighbor. But we did see the source of our woes. A round, curved disk floated like a little steel ship on the water inside the closet. It was about as big around as one of those snow disks you use to careen down a wintry slope.

The bottom of our water heater.

Dad explained, "It looks like it simply rusted out. It got so corroded that the whole seam just let loose."

I said, "Too bad it hasn't learned how to hold its water."

Smart-mouth kid. Everyone groaned.

Dad continued, "The pipe that refills the tank when it goes down hasn't gotten the message that there is no bottom in the heater, so it's just doing its job like it's supposed to."

Everyone looked at me, waiting for another wisecrack.

I just looked surprised and said, "What? I'm just listening."

"Lucky for us the house isn't watertight," Dad added.

"Why's that?" we all asked at the same time.

"Well, the pipe would have continued to fill up what it thought was the tank until the water level was about five feet high, when a float would have finally stopped it."

"That would have been awesome," I said.

They all looked at me again.

"Well. It would have."

"Lucky for us," Dad summed up, "our back door doesn't seal very well at the threshold, so I'll bet most of the excess water is seeping out the back door, onto the patio, and out into the backyard."

"Guess we won't have to use the sprinkler for a few days, huh?" I said.

Though very tired, and in a vulnerable state of mind, Dad surprised us all. He began barking orders like a captain directing his crew. His brisk good humor in that situation was infectious.

"You, first mate," he said, pointing at me, "grab a towel from the bathroom and start swabbing the deck."

"Aye, aye, Cap'n. But where's the deck?"

"Uh, the bathroom," he said. "Start sopping up the water in the bathroom and wring out the towel into the toilet, because that will carry the water down below the floor level."

I saluted and stumped off, peg-leg style, toward the bathroom.

"You, helmsman," he said, pointing to my sister, "grab the keys to the toolshed. I'll head to the backyard to retrieve the tools necessary to fix the pipe."

And to my mother he said (in a much less demanding tone), "Dear, would you mind getting the flashlight so I can see to turn off the water?"

I guess he had either run out of nautical terms or he was being extra polite with Mom. He must have known that it's always better to ask nicely when it comes to your wife.

Considering the lateness of the hour and the tiredness of all the crew, it could have been a much stickier, much more unhappy situation than it really was. We could have all been totally disgusted with the whole thing, sniping at each other, and sloshing around in our soaking-wet attitudes for days.

But thanks to my Dad's attitude toward it all, the detour turned into a family adventure. None of us will ever forget it.

There we were, on our soaking-wet knees, wringing out bath towels into the toilets in both bathrooms, singing, in harmony, "There shall be showers of blessing."

Dad did the right thing, and it amazes me as I look back on that situation. He laughed off what couldn't be changed and set us all to work...together.

Our little adventure up Water Heater Creek revealed to me that leaks in life just happen.

Leaky water heaters happen.

Leaky radiator hoses happen.

Leaky diapers happen (sometimes on your good clothes right before you leave for a special evening).

And often, it's nobody's fault.

Dad's water heater didn't cook up a scheme to see how far over the emotional edge it could push my dad after a long, hard day. It didn't hide in the hall closet, whispering to its cousin, the air conditioner, "Psst. Hey, A.C. Listen up. It's all set. It's goin' down tonight. At precisely 8:34. That's when I'm going to drop the bottom out of my tank and flood the joint. It's the perfect time, because the owners will be gone all day. Boy, will they get what's coming to them when *they* get home."

Sometimes, the way we react to life's little leaks (and some of the big ones), you'd think inanimate objects had minds of their own. But they don't.

My dad recognized that what Chuck Swindoll says is true: "Life is 10 percent what happens to you and 90 percent how you respond to it."

He's as right as rain.

My rule of thumb, after our anchor-dropping, bilge-pumping evening, is this: *If the detour doesn't involve the loss of life or limb, and if it's only water you hear dripping—not blood—then laugh it off.*

Change what's changeable, and laugh off the rest. Hey, it worked for Dad, and it rubbed off on the rest of us that night.

From the kitchen, my mom hollered, "Boy, ya know, when it rains it pours."

Then, from the back bathroom, Dad replied, "You know what they say. The rain falls on the just as well as the unjust."

Kathey got into the act by saying, "Dad, have you been playing with that Moses staff again? Remember, you're only supposed to strike the rock *once.*"

I called from the other bathroom, "I bet I know who caused this flood."

"Who?" both Dad and Kathey shot back.

"Farrah *Faucet.*"

We joked and laughed, squeegeed and splashed, wrung

and flushed, until our sides hurt. Then we crawled into bed, even though there was still much to do.

The next day, with the help of our handy-dandy carpenter friend and next-door neighbor, Dad tore the carpet out. The insurance company came to assess the damage, and within six weeks, the aroma of rotting carpet padding was replaced by the smell of beautiful new wall-to-wall carpet.

Mom had always wanted carpet all through the living room and down the hall. She wouldn't have chosen a flood to get it. But it worked out. We even salvaged enough carpet from the preflood days to put carpet in my sister's room.

I wish all my detours had been this fun. Obviously, some detours are not a laughing matter. You can't simply laugh away the pain of a serious loss, especially if human life is involved. But many of the detours in life—the terribly inconvenient, totally unexpected ones—come along simply because things wear out, break, or fall apart in this imperfect, fallen world we occupy.

And when that has happened in my life, I've found it has been much more smooth sailing when I've remembered to change what's changeable, and laugh away the rest.

I had to remind myself of that fact when my wife and I discovered a post-rainstorm basement in our Michigan home. There was enough water in there to start a shrimp farm.

Oh sure, we were frustrated, and we dealt with the normal emotions of vexation, just like anyone would. But we kept reminding ourselves that it was only stuff. Stuff breaks. Stuff wears out. But it's still just *stuff*.

Life's not worth getting too bent out of shape over stuff.

So, I'm going to try real hard to remember my own advice

the next time we have a hard spring thaw followed by a rain-storm. The next time I step into a basement that looks like the municipal wading pool, I'll do what I can to solve the problem.

And as we each grab a tin can and start to bail, I'll start singing, "Shall we gather at the river?"

CHAPTER SEVEN

A Hard Lesson in Grace

I stood on the brake.

We heard the sound of skidding tires. Our tires. But the skidding didn't last very long. With the sickening sounds of crumpling metal and breaking glass, our car slammed into the back end of the car ahead.

Then, suddenly everything was still.

For a moment we both just sat there, stunned. We began taking inventory. Apparently no broken bones. My seat belt had kept me from slamming into the steering wheel, and I was only a little sore where the belt crossed my shoulder.

Joy was holding her knees. They had broken out the air-conditioning vents on the dashboard. But she wasn't bleeding. Only bruised.

Then it struck me, as hard as I had just struck the car in front of me: *I've just ruined our plans to drive to Michigan and get married.* In such split seconds as those, detours begin.

I had met Joy in a singing class called oratorio, a sort of junior varsity choir at Grand Canyon College (now University). She sat in the front row with the altos. I was perched high up on the risers in the back with the tenors.

Every time she glanced back in my direction, I'd quickly turn my head in another direction, or look at my music, so she wouldn't catch me staring at her lovely, long hair. Ahhh. That hair. Always clean and shiny. And feathered all the way down the sides. Very fashionable for 1976.

This girl was a vision. And this boy had never been so smitten in all of his life.

My parents had prepared me for fiscal responsibility before I went to college. Dad had laid down the law. "As long as you stay in school full time and live at home, we'll pay for your tuition. But if you decide it's time to move out on your own, then it'll be time for you to pay your own way. Deal?"

I had agreed, because I'd never imagined meeting a girl who would sweep me so completely off my feet in only my second year of college. Dreams, after all, are just dreams. How could a guy anticipate a dream walking into his college classroom and carrying him away? It was a blindside.

Up to that point, I'd been a serious student who got good grades, applied himself to his studies at night, and enjoyed playing Frisbee with his buddies between classes. Romance 'n' marriage? That could wait.

But then *she* showed up in that front row of oratorio. It was like one of those corny songs on the oldies station. I couldn't keep my eyes off her. I just had to meet her; but how? I didn't even know her name. And it didn't appear that she had any friends who knew any of my friends. I certainly wasn't about to just walk up to her and stick out my hand and say, "Hello. I've wanted to introduce myself." That would *never* work.

For one thing, she seemed way out of my league. And for another, I scored a whopping two on a scale from one to ten in self-confidence.

Then, one golden October morning, I was walking to music history class when I saw my sister, Kathey, talking with Joy on the front steps to Fleming Hall. *Yes!* I thought. *This is my chance. Oh, bless you, Kathey Cothern.*

Heart pounding, I walked up and said in the most casual voice I could manage, "Hi, Kath. I see you're busy studying for that next exam."

She gave me a fake punch on my shoulder and said, "Yeah, yeah, you know me. Always putting the old nose to the grindstone."

I glanced over and smiled at Joy, who was obviously waiting for an introduction. I looked back at Kathey. *C'mon, girl, don't let me down now.*

She didn't.

"Oh," she said, "um, I'd like to introduce you to my new friend, Joy. This is my 'little' brother, Clark," and she held her hand up to show that I was eight inches taller than she was.

That was that. Now that we were properly introduced, it became easier to strike up conversations before and after class. A week later I even worked up enough courage to ask her out for a double date.

Larkin, my trumpet-playing band buddy, agreed to go with us. He was going to take his girlfriend, and the four of us were going to see a movie. I liked that idea. (Safety in numbers, and all that.) Besides, Larkin always knew how to keep the conversation going, so if I got mealy-mouthed and tongue-tied, he could keep things lively.

Then, just an hour before we were supposed to leave, Larkin called to say that his girlfriend was sick. He said, "Why don't you just go ahead and take Joy. I'm sure she'd like that."

Oh, man.

I was scared to death. But my desire to get to know her better overwhelmed my desire to join the Foreign Legion, so I called her.

And she agreed.

We drove across town and saw *The Good-bye Girl* and then ate some dinner. I don't think I said more than six words during the entire movie. But afterward, over supper, the conversation finally began to flow. Boy, did it flow. I'd never been able to talk about so many things with a girl in my entire life. We had so much in common: church backgrounds, similar tastes in music, experience in musical ministry groups while in high school; the list seemed to go on and on.

After dinner, on the way home, Joy said, "Uh, I have something to confess."

Uh-oh. Those are frightening words to a guy on his first date. I'd heard those same words before, right before that cute brunette told me she was engaged to someone else and had only gone out with me because she didn't want to hurt my feelings.

My stomach tightened, and I said (as casually as I could manage), "Oh?"

She said, "Well, you remember when we were first introduced? On the steps to Fleming?"

How could I forget? The angels had sung. Rays of sunlight had come streaming through the clouds to illuminate the very spot where we were standing. "Yeah, I remember," I said.

"Well, I sort of introduced myself to your sister right before you got there, because I knew you had to walk right by there to get to your next class. I'd kind of been watching you and wanting to meet you."

This was not at all what I'd expected her to say. Wow!

She continued, "You seem so confident with all your friends. You have such a great sense of humor. But I thought you just didn't want to meet me. I kept trying to catch your attention after oratorio, but you were always out the door before I could find you. So I took matters into my own hands."

Diabolical.

I loved this girl! My confidence soared like a bottle rocket.

I arrived home that first evening, and after only one date, I just *knew* Joy was The One For Me. Of course, I thought I'd "known" that before, with a couple other girls I'd dated, and...well, I'd been wrong. But *this* time it was different. I didn't know how I knew. I just knew. I knew I knew I knew.

I wrote on my calendar, "This is the one." (I didn't tell her that until much later, not wanting to scare her away.)

Suddenly, Joy was the sun and I was the earth. (Or was it the earth and the moon? Neptune and Pluto?) Anyway, my life began revolving around Joy. My fervent focus on my studies shifted to a fervent focus on her. I spent my evenings over at her grandparents' home, where I could be around her. I could hardly sleep, wasn't eating well, and my preoccupation with "that girl" became all too obvious to my parents.

Looking back at my behavior, I can see now that I must have increased the intensity of their prayer life dramatically. I'm sure that their sleep habits were interrupted too, the moment after I announced to them that I had found "a really wonderful girl."

And she really was (and is). But even with all her positive, endearing qualities, both my mother and father were convinced I was falling too hard, too fast. One night at dinner they told me, "Clark, listen. If you have any plans for marriage, we feel you should wait until after you graduate from college. You really have to plan ahead before jumping into a lifelong commitment."

And Dad said, "Remember our deal."

It wasn't a question. It was an ultimatum. His words from nearly two years earlier began to haunt me: "When you are mature enough to get married or move away from home, you are also mature enough to pay your own way."

I tried, I really did. I studied. I threw myself into the books again…but Joy's face seemed to be on every page. When I wasn't with her, I was missing her. If I could have been in her presence twenty-four hours a day, I would have. But as that relationship heated up, my normally close relationship with my parents became increasingly strained. I had jumped off the road of a great relationship with Mom and Dad and had begun a bumpy ride down a path of self-absorption and irrational behavior.

Though we didn't have any knock-down-drag-out fights, I do remember some very tense discussions, all of which left my parents (and me) tied in knots. Some nights I just drove around until after midnight, trying to sort out my thoughts. I didn't know it at the time, but my parents thought I was spending all that time with Joy. Actually, Joy's grandmother took her role as chaperone very seriously. She made sure I had Joy home at a reasonable hour. Grammy, as we called her, would look at the clock at about 10 P.M. and say, in a tone that would slice through bricks, "*Mister* Cothern. It's time for any *respectable* young man to be leaving."

At first, Grammy's demeanor scared me to death. But as I got to know her better, I would tease back, "Don't hold back, Grammy; tell me how you *really* feel."

I knew, and Joy knew, and Grammy knew that Joy and I hadn't been doing anything wrong. But my parents had no way of knowing that when I pulled into the driveway at one in the morning.

One night, in a tense showdown, my parents and I got as close as ever to the fork in the road. We were all about one badly worded sentence away from a major parting of the ways.

I told them, "I believe Joy is the person God has chosen to be with me for the rest of my life. If you try to stand in our way, then you're standing in the way of God's will for my life."

I can't believe I said that, but I did. Even now, to write those words, is like a punch in the gut. These were the parents who had always loved me and tried to do what was best for my safety and well-being. These were the parents who were paying my tuition, at real personal sacrifice. It was certainly a stupid way to act. And to think I, who had acted with such immaturity, was preaching to my father, the preacher, telling *him* that *he* was standing in the way of God's will. Ugh.

If it hurts me this badly this many years later, I'm sure it must have been devastating to my parents. But at the time I was so blinded by infatuation that I only saw what I wanted to see.

It's amazing my parents didn't plant their feet squarely on my backside and just kick me out after I'd treated them that way. But they didn't. They acted with tremendous self-restraint.

I remember my dad saying with a deep sigh, "Clark, we're just concerned about you and your health—and about your college education. If Joy is the right girl for you, then listen, son, she'll *still* be the right one after you graduate from college. It's in the Lord's hands. And then—after college—you'll have a better chance to get a decent job and support your new family. For something as important as this, two and a half years isn't too long to wait."

Two and a half *years?* He might as well have said two and a half centuries. It was intolerable.

Mom said, "It's not that we don't like Joy. She's a lovely young lady. I'm just afraid you're losing sight of your educational goals."

Then she said something that really hurt. But the reason it hurt was because deep down, I knew it was true.

"I'm just afraid that if you drop out of school now and get married, you'll never finish, and you'll wind up digging ditches for a living."

There it was. She'd laid her true feelings right on the table. My mother was afraid I would have to resort to manual labor to support my wife. Well, I wasn't afraid to work hard. I knew what I was capable of doing, and even if I had to work full time *and* go to school, I could finish. I'd show them.

I took a long walk after that. About eight miles, round trip. I remember saying to myself, *I hate this stupid tug-of-war. I love my parents, but I also love Joy. Why can't they see that?*

That very night, I decided to pop the question.

It was time for a showdown.

That's what I kept telling myself. It was either all or nothin'. My timing or no timing. My schedule or bag the whole deal. In that infatuation-induced state of mind, I felt I needed to make a clean break from the old apron strings and start a new life with the young woman I knew was right for me.

Later that week, I asked Joy to marry me. She accepted, not knowing the tremendous strain I was placing on my parents.

Soon after that, in late spring, Joy and I announced our official engagement as my parents sat, stone faced and sullen. My father said something like, "Though we have told you how we feel about the timing of this event, we want you to know that as your parents we will support you in your decision, since it's obvious you intend to go through with this. We won't do anything to jeopardize your relationship."

But they weren't jumping up and down about it, either.

It certainly wasn't the kind of unconditional blessing I had hoped for, but looking back, I can see now that my parents were acting as graciously as possible after the way I'd treated them.

Joy and I made plans to drive from Arizona to Michigan, where Joy's parents lived, for the wedding later that summer. My parents did the best they could to act supportive, though I knew from the antacids they were popping that they were churning inside.

Living in the same house with them was becoming increasingly difficult. I tried to avoid seeing them as much as possible and spent as much time with Joy as I could.

The evening before our scheduled trip to Michigan, we were headed to my parents' home from the college where we had said good-bye to a couple of friends. Joy sat in the passenger side of my little yellow Subaru. I kept looking over at her, flashing goofy looks and smiling, excited for our upcoming trip and marriage.

As I shot through a busy intersection, I glanced at the light, saw that it was turning yellow, then looked over at Joy. I was so grateful that in just a few weeks, we would be together, as man and wife, for the rest of our lives. When I looked back in front of me, I saw that the car that had been traveling quickly through the intersection had suddenly stopped.

That's when my personal plans for our trip to Michigan exploded in a wreck.

I have just blown it, I thought. *Man, I have royally, totally blown this whole deal.* I just knew all our plans for the upcoming trip and wedding were ruined.

If I hadn't been goo-goo-eyeing Joy, I probably would have been more alert and could have avoided the accident. The truth was, I'd been so blinded by my infatuation and growing love for her that I'd missed seeing a lot of things around me. Including my parents' love, which had been expressed by their concern over the timing of my marriage.

Besides Joy's knees and my ego being badly bruised, no one was seriously hurt in the accident. Apparently the car in front of us had stopped unexpectedly because the car in front of them had decided to turn left, from the wrong lane, into an apartment complex.

After giving the police officer who arrived at the scene all the necessary information, we started back toward my parents' house. Our little Subaru still ran, but it looked as if we'd just bought it from a junkyard. The hood was crumpled, both headlights were broken out, and the left front fender was badly bent. What used to be a grill was now a tangle of broken plastic, with gaps of the radiator showing through like a hockey player's smile.

After driving only a mile down the road, the shock suddenly kicked in. Compounding that, all the events and tension of the past few weeks spilled over and I began to cry uncontrollably. I had to pull the car over. I put my head on Joy's shoulder and wept.

A dozen questions raced through my mind. *Have I been acting selfishly lately? Were my parents right? Should I have waited to get married? Have I just ruined our chances to get to Michigan? Was this some sort of test? Maybe a punishment for the way I've behaved? How will my parents feel about me now that I've wrecked my car?*

Devastated by the accident, I asked Joy, "Do you think we should call off the wedding for now?"

She said, "Let's talk about it when we get back to your parents' house."

When I finally regained my composure, I drove the rest of the way home, knowing I still had to face my parents. In my mind, I imagined my father giving me the famous "I told you so" speech. I certainly deserved it. He would have been completely justified to angrily drive home the point that I had been acting like a selfish, impetuous brat. I braced myself for the blistering reaction I had imagined.

I pulled into the driveway and stopped the wrecked car. Joy gave me one last approving hug, providing a shot of the courage I didn't have, and we walked into the house to face my parents.

Seeing that they were on the back patio, I walked through the door and before I could say anything about the accident, I broke into tears again, this time feeling incredible remorse for the way I had treated them in the past few weeks. They could tell something was seriously wrong.

My mother reacted first by walking over to hug me as I cried. Mom and Dad waited patiently as I blubbered out the news of our accident. They hugged Joy, too, and asked if she was okay.

Then they surprised me. Neither of them said a word about my behavior in the past weeks. Instead Mom said, "We're just glad neither of you was hurt badly or killed."

Dad added, "That's right. Cars can be replaced. They're just things. We're glad *you're* okay."

He never said a thing about the way I'd been acting lately. Not one word. I think he and Mom could both tell that I was feeling terrible about the whole series of events.

Dad walked out to survey the damage to the car, looked it over carefully, and then said, "You know, I'll bet Jerry, the body shop guy, could probably bump the fenders and hood back into fairly good shape without having to get new parts. It won't cost you very much, if you don't mind driving a car that doesn't look perfect. That way you could pay for it without having to go through the insurance company. It would also keep your rates from going sky high.

"Then," he added, "you could still get to Michigan. It

might set your schedule back by a week or two, but I'll bet you could still make it in time for that wedding."

Wedding? I couldn't believe it. Dad was actually helping us plan to get to Michigan and still have the wedding!

That night was a turning point in the way I treated my parents. I started to see that, though I had not considered their feelings, they had been considering mine all along. Two weeks after the accident we drove to Michigan, along with a passenger, Joy's mother. She had flown down to act as chaperone.

In August, Mom sat crying as my sister Kathey sang for our wedding. Dad stood next to the minister from Joy's former church. My father pronounced us man and wife.

Ironically, one of the first jobs I held after our marriage involved (are you ready for this?) digging ditches. I worked for a plumber friend of mine, who handed me a shovel on the first hour of the first day and said, "Dig from here to there, about twelve inches deep. Have fun."

My mother's words rang in my ears with every shovelful of dirt: "We're just worried that you'll have to dig ditches for a living if you get married before you finish college."

But I applied myself. If I had to dig ditches to provide for my new wife, then I'd do the best I could. I'd do it with all my strength. It was good, honest work, and I'd do whatever it took.

Dad and Mom held true to our deal. We were on our own financially.

It wasn't long, though, until Joy got a job working in the business office at the college, allowing me to go back to school tuition free. Joy worked very hard to put me through the rest of my bachelor's degree. And then, when I felt called to attend seminary, she worked even harder to put me through my master's program.

My mother was still concerned that we might have a baby too soon and that a child early in our lives would disrupt my education. She mentioned this to Joy on more than one occasion.

After one such time, Joy finally looked Mom right in the eyes and said, "I'll tell you what, Mom. You just let us know when you're ready for us to give you a grandchild, and we'll see what we can do."

Six years after our marriage, after we'd moved from Phoenix to Fort Worth, Texas, so I could attend seminary, we received a box in the mail from my parents. In it were three Christmas stockings, two big ones with the names "Joy" and "Clark" written in glue and glitter, and one tiny stocking with the word "Baby" on top. Sticking out of the little stocking was a note. It said simply, "Anytime now would be just fine."

It was my mother's creative way of saying, "Sorry for being overprotective. I'm backing off. I'll let you get on with your life as a couple now."

Seven and a half years after our wedding, our first child was born. Katheryn came along just six weeks before I graduated from seminary, and eight weeks before Christmas. My parents drove all the way from Phoenix to see little Katie and to spend Christmas with us. They were thrilled with our little family. We have a photograph of my Dad holding baby Katie, with me in the background, dressed in my graduation gown. It was truly commencement day in more ways than one.

We had all graduated to a new level of respect in our relationship.

Both my mother and father repeatedly told Joy and continue to tell her, "We're so proud of you. We see that you really *are* the one God had in store for Clark, and we couldn't have chosen a better 'other daughter' if we had tried."

Now that all three of our children are in school all day, Joy has gone back to school part time to finish her bachelor's degree, something she gave up when she went to work to put me through school. My parents are paying for Joy's tuition. (Joy's earning wonderful grades, too.)

Two summers ago, we shared a family vacation with my mom and dad in Colorado, retracing the steps of an earlier vacation when I was a kid. Joy helped my dad in and out of the van since he was stiff with Parkinson's disease. I saw the twinkle in his eye that showed how much he adores Joy. We have some memorable photos from that vacation, with three generations of Botherns all getting along well and loving one another.

Joy and I celebrated our twentieth wedding anniversary in August of '98. It's an event my parents weren't sure would ever happen back when I dropped out of college to marry *that* girl. I don't know that we would have made it this far either if they hadn't continued to offer their support to us, even though I had made some very immature decisions early on.

When I wrecked the car I realized that I had almost made a wreck of my relationship with my parents. Fortunately, amazingly, they acted as God acts toward me all the time. Even when I blow it by running impetuously ahead of Him, He's still there, waiting to pick up the pieces and point me in the right direction for the future.

If I could press a rewind button and do it all over again, I would probably have waited to get married until both Joy and

I had finished college. But since I can't, I remain grateful that my parents and I grew through the years, and that we came out the other side of that bumpy side-road detour stronger than when we went in.

Some detours, by God's grace, are like that.

CHAPTER EIGHT

Out of Control
at the Post Office

U h-oh."

I watched the very tall, wide-shouldered man straighten up after unfolding himself from his car. As he walked toward me, I thought, *This guy's going to punch me right in the face.*

What's sad is that I deserved it.

Earlier that cloudy Wednesday afternoon a little fellow named Matthew had walked up to the edge of the snow runoff ditch behind his parents' mobile home where he stood, staring at the icy water, upon which floated chunks of snow and pieces of tree bark. Captivated by the objects swiftly rushing by, only inches from his toes, Matthew became entranced by the hypnotic motion of the stream.

Matthew, his older brother, and his two cousins ignored the low forties temperature on that November Michigan afternoon. They cranked up their little body thermostats by staying as busy as preschoolers can—running, swinging, chasing each other, and chucking rocks into the stream.

It was Matthew's third birthday.

Joy and I were his neighbors, though we had only seen his family enough to wave hello as we passed them on our narrow mobile-home park street. At the time, we lived in Whitmore Lake since I was working as the minister of education and music at a church in Ann Arbor, a fifteen-minute drive away.

Matthew's parents had ducked inside their home for a couple of minutes when, without warning, little Matthew either fell in, walked in, or the snow under Matthew's feet gave way and he slipped into the ditch and was quickly swept downstream by the current. The other kids watched helplessly as his head disappeared under the icy water. They ran inside to tell Matthew's folks, but it was too late.

Matthew was gone.

Another neighbor, friends of Matthew's family, knocked on our door and poured out the tragic news between heartbreaking sobs.

"We don't know if he was reaching for a toy that got thrown into the water or if he just got too close to the edge. All we know is, rescue workers couldn't find him right away. It took them ten minutes to get here, and then another twenty-five before they found his little body a quarter of a mile downstream. They're treating him as a cold-water drowning, and there's still a slight chance the water was cold enough to lower his body temperature and slow his heart rate. But...he was without oxygen for so long."

Not knowing the family that well, Joy and I weren't sure what to do. But if our presence at the hospital might yield some comfort—any comfort at all—well, it was worth the trip.

That's how some detours begin.

Suddenly, someone else's crisis drops an opportunity for ministry right into your lap, with no time to prepare, no time to think it through. I can see why the apostle Paul said, "Be prepared in season and out of season" (2 Timothy 4:2).

We thought we could at least offer to help with some of the practical things that might be needed, calling relatives, driving someone to someone else's house. Whatever. We had no idea what they would be facing.

We made the twenty-minute drive from Whitmore Lake into Ann Arbor to the University of Michigan Mott's Children's Hospital. All the way there we kept saying, "Lord, how do we pray at a time like this?" I couldn't help but think, *What if that were our child? How would I feel? How can we possibly do anything to help?*

A neighbor saw us coming down the hall toward the ICU waiting room and quickly got a message to Matthew's parents. They said, "A minister's here. Do you want him to pray for Matt?"

Quite suddenly, before we even had a chance to talk with any of the gathering crowd, someone took me by the elbow and ushered me right into the Intensive Care Unit. I found myself gazing at a lifeless-looking little boy with a bloated stomach, blue lips, and more tubes and wires than I've seen attached to a human before. I tried to look more concerned than shocked, but the sight wasn't one I was used to seeing— and pray I never have to see again.

His stomach and chest rose and fell to the rhythm of the noisy ventilator, whooshing and hissing with each new breath. His skin seemed so pale, especially under the glow of the bright lights, used in part to see well enough to insert needles into tiny veins, and in part to warm his little body.

Knowing how many minutes little Matthew had been without oxygen, a thought shoved its way past my faith and into my brain. *It would be a miracle for this little guy to survive.* Matt's mom and dad looked as though they'd aged ten years in two hours. They looked at me with eyes that pleaded for help. They didn't have to say a word. I could tell they were grasping for any shred of hope.

I felt oddly detached from the situation; these people were almost strangers to me. Though I was standing in the same place, looking at the same little boy, I also found myself looking at the whole situation objectively, as an outside observer who had been drawn inside the intimate circle of a painful circumstance. I thought, *Wow, these people need a professional.*

Then, realizing they were looking to me for help, I thought, *Oh, man. They think I'M a professional.* But no matter how many courses you take in counseling or hospital visitation ministry, nothing can quite prepare you for this kind of ordeal. I was so used to feeling in control. But this whole situation was completely out of my hands. I had no control over this tragedy whatsoever.

My face masking my inadequacy, I asked Matt's parents, "What have the doctors told you?"

They told me what I already knew. All the same, I felt it might be good for them to tell someone else, if for no other reason than to cement the truth of the situation in minds as numb and as murky with grief as that runoff ditch's water.

Matt's dad said, "None of the doctors are givin' us any signs of hope."

At these words, Matt's mom shut her eyes tightly and turned her head the other way, obviously applying every ounce of strength to keep from completely falling apart. Though I was barely ten years older than both of them, they looked far too young and too helpless to be facing such a tragedy. My heart broke for them. I knew I would be absolutely crushed if this were my child lying before me. I also knew that, though I believed God was capable of healing miracles, I had never personally experienced one—not with me as the central character in the prayer drama.

I wanted to *will* Matt back to life, but I knew only God was capable of that. I also knew that God, knowing what's best in the long run, can choose not to heal. But these parents didn't want any theological explanations just then.

They just wanted their little boy to live.

I asked, "Would you mind if I prayed for little Matthew?" I knew they wouldn't, but it felt like the right thing to do, to ask first. They nodded, and Matt's mom instinctively reached out and grabbed Matt's right hand in both of hers, preparing for what I knew must be her last attempt to revive him. She didn't say a word. She just looked at me, and then back at Matt. When I bowed my head, they bowed theirs too, as though following my lead.

In less than a second another thought crept in from somewhere and struck me. I thought, *This is an odd situation. These folks don't darken the door of any church. As far as I know, they don't even like to talk about spiritual things, yet WHAM, this terrible thing happens to their son and they are practically begging God to do something.*

In a nanosecond, I chastised myself for even thinking such

a pompous, self-righteous thought. I knew that often these types of tragedies grab people's attention and drive them to their knees, where they finally see that God was there all along. Besides, I really didn't resent being called on to pray for the little fellow. I would have been grateful for any kind of help if I were in their shoes. My presence in the room provided a strange sense of purpose for them, because I represented God's presence. (What an awesome, frightening thought that is.)

I quickly modified my internal reasoning. *I'm really no different than these people, am I? It's easy for me to want to talk with God only when I really need something. Then, when things get bad, there I am, banging on His door, asking for Him to do things my way. These people and I, we're not so different at the core.*

Remembering that thought made it easier to be grateful for the open doors tragedy provided. So in the next breath, as I inhaled, preparing to offer a plea for God's help, I prayed to myself, *Lord, help me to say Your words, and give Your support. Help me to give hope, but not false hope. Please speak through me. They need to know You're here, even though You might not answer their prayers in the way they would like.*

In that one instant, a multitude of feelings hit me all at once. I felt nervous, humbled, dependent upon God, and sort of like I did on that crazy opening night of *The Wizard of Oz* back in high school. I didn't want to mess up, because people were counting on me to say the right words. I acted confident on the outside, waiting for the feelings to catch up, but inside my stomach was twisting itself into a pretzel. No one had written me a script for this scene back in drama class. And seminary training was only theory.

This was the real thing.

I took hold of the only thing on Matthew's bloated little body that wasn't connected to some sort of electrode, needle, tube, or machine—a tiny toe on his right foot. Then I prayed softly, out loud, "God, You know what's best for little Matthew. You know him and love him better than any of us possibly can, and that's quite a lot."

Matt's mother sniffled, trying not to burst out crying.

I continued, "Because You know what's best, we trust You, even when we can't trust our own emotions. We trust that if he's better off with You, You will spare him the pain and suffering he would endure here if he were to live."

I knew that would be hard for them to hear, yet I felt I had to pray it. Then, as though not wanting to rule out a genuine miracle, I added, "Yet, if You choose to heal his little body, we know You can do that too, so we trust if that's best for Matthew, You'll heal him and bring him back to us. Either way, Lord, we trust You to do what You know is best. I know You understand the kind of suffering and grief this family is going through because of what *Your* Son went through...and I know You are hurting right along with these people right now. Please give them comfort by becoming real to them. Show them Your presence."

And I longed for my last sentence to be true.

I paused for just a moment, wondering if I should pray any more, but after a deep breath, decided I'd said enough. I closed with, "In Jesus' name I pray. Amen."

I raised my head and my eyes met the eyes of Matthew's parents. They looked pleadingly at me, then at their son, who looked as lifeless as before the prayer. We all paused for an eternal five seconds, just watching Matthew.

Breaking the uncomfortable silence, I began shaking the hands of these distraught parents. I whispered, "Please let me know if there is anything at all we can do to help. I wish I could do more. I'm so, *so* sorry you're going through this."

I hoped something in my brief prayer had helped. The family seemed grateful that I had come. They both half-whispered, half-cried, "Thank you," and I walked out of ICU into the waiting room thinking, *Lord, help them not to be angry at You if Matthew doesn't make it.*

Matthew was pronounced dead a short time later that afternoon.

I didn't know if ministers were supposed to feel what I was feeling just then. Tired. Upset. Helpless. Frustrated. Sad. Lonely. Depressed.

I didn't feel much like going to church to conduct our mid-week choir rehearsal. Since we were preparing for our upcoming Christmas musical, we would be singing about angels bringing good tidings of great joy. And considering the announcement I'd just received from the hospital, I didn't feel very joyful.

But I was committed to that choir. Besides, that's what I was getting paid to do. *C'mon, Clark,* I told myself. *Get a grip. Duty awaits.* Joy and I didn't have enough time to drive back to our mobile home, so we decided to swing by the post office to mail some letters and then go on to church. Freezing rain had begun to fall, and the sky looked as miserable and cold as I felt in my heart.

I swung into the drive-thru at the main branch of the post office off Stadium Boulevard and pulled in behind another car. It paused at the first box marked "Local" and then pulled ahead about one car length to the "Out of Town." In my rearview mirror, I watched two other cars turn in off of Stadium, pulling up right behind me. Assuming the driver of the car in front had completed his task, I pulled up as close as I could to his rear bumper to make room for the cars behind.

That's when the fellow in the car just ahead decided he needed to back up to the box he'd just passed. Evidently he still had some local letters to mail. But what could I do? I was stuck.

His back-up lights went on and he began edging back.

I looked at his back-up lights and said, "What is this guy trying to do?"

He honked. Honked! *At me.*

I fumed.

He honked again and started inching his car farther back toward mine. I checked my mirror. Another car had pulled up behind us, so we were really piling up in the driveway.

Great. Just great, I thought. *Here I am caught right in the middle of an impossible situation. I can't go forward, can't go backward. I can't seem to do anything!*

It was just then that the rear bumper of the car in front bumped the front bumper of my car. Though I wasn't aware of it at the time, my odd predicament reflected my overall sense of frustration. I had been powerless to keep Matthew from dying, and I was powerless here to effect any change of any kind. I was absolutely, totally, completely incapable of doing *anything* to change the situation.

Despite the falling temperature outside, I boiled over.

Joy, sensing my rising blood pressure, patted me on the knee and said, "Honey. It's *okay*. There's nothing you can do."

Oh yeah? I thought, ignoring her. *There is TOO something I can do, watch THIS!*

Rolling down my window, feeling the icy blast of wind and the freezing drops of rain sting my face, I hollered—no, screamed—as loudly as I could, and pronouncing each word slowly, for added emphasis, "Move—your—car!"

In the heat of passion, as those words were being hurled from my mouth, I felt strangely better. What a release, to be able to unload on someone.

That feeling was short-lived.

Two seconds after the last word left my mouth and landed on the ear of the driver in front, I realized it probably would have been prudent to check the height, weight, fist size, and athletic ability of the phantom driver *before* using my outdoor voice on a total stranger.

He was big. *Really* big. And as he strolled back toward my car, I shrank in my seat. "Oh, man," I said, bracing myself for a seriously painful punch in the face. I wondered if our health insurance covered plastic surgery.

Joy must have looked really nervous sitting next to me, because the man just looked at me for a moment. He never even reached in and grabbed me by the throat.

Realizing that I was still in one piece, and that this man was just standing there, awaiting some explanation, I offered a feeble, "I'm sorry, it's just that, well, you have no idea the kind of day I've had today."

Even to myself, as the words crawled out of my mouth,

they didn't sound very convincing. In fact, what I just offered this man in return for his dignity (which I had just insulted), was a really lame excuse for acting like I had just acted. But it was the only thing I could think of on such short notice.

He looked at me for a second and then said, "Well, don't take it out on a total stranger like you'd take it out on your kids."

Ouch. I grimaced.

That hurt. His statement stung worse, in some ways, than a punch in the nose. He was right. I had no right to take out my frustration on anyone, stranger or not. I sat there, humiliated. And grateful.

He took a step over to the "local" box, slipped in his remaining letters, sauntered slowly back to his car, got in, and drove away. I was afraid to look at Joy. When I finally did, she just gave me one of those Mona Lisa half smiles and shook her head. I heard what she was saying, even though she didn't utter a word. She was telling me, "You, my skinny little husband, are one *mighty* lucky fellow. And it's just a good thing he didn't know you were a minister."

I took a deep breath, rubbed my eyes with my hands, and answered her look, "I know, I know." And drove us to church.

I discovered a thing or two on this detour through the post office drive-thru. Just about the time I thought I was all prepared for the many expectations of ministry to others, I was shown that, despite terrible circumstances, God's still in charge.

I'm not.

He's still very adequate.

I'm totally inadequate.

And despite what I knew to be true about Him, I still tried to handle someone else's crisis as though I were somehow capable of doing something to change the outcome. As though I were somehow in control. And yet, I had never felt more *out* of control than in that ICU ward.

I had taken the pain of someone else's tragedy so personally that I forgot to hand those grieving people over into the Father's care.

I felt that afternoon very much like good old King David, who said:

The cords of death entangled me,
the anguish of the grave came upon me;
I was overcome by trouble and sorrow.
(Psalm 116:3)

I hear you, man. I too was overcome. Totally.

But you know what else I learned in the middle of that detour? I learned that, despite my faithless behavior, God remains absolutely faithful. After my pressure-cooker emotions blew their top, I had called on the name of the Lord, just like David had.

He and I had both cried, "O Lord, save me!"

And fortunately, the Lord who was so good to David when *he* was feeling like I felt that day—the same Lord who was with me in that car at the post office—was "gracious and...full of compassion." I was so relieved that "the LORD protects the simplehearted; when I was in great need, he saved me" (Psalm 116:5, 6).

For some very human reasons, I thought that everybody

expected me to remain totally unmoved by the experience back at the hospital, because I was a "professional minister," rock solid in my faith. But I realized that no matter what other people expected of me, I was still pretty darned vulnerable to other people's pain, and that God still had some character building to do in my life.

Fortunately for me, He heard my whimpering voice in the car that afternoon. "He heard my cry for mercy."

I'll be forever grateful.

"Because he turned his ear to me, I will call on him as long as I live" (Psalm 116:1, 2).

Choir rehearsal was canceled that night. By the time our Wednesday-night prayer meeting had finished, the roads were getting so slippery with continual freezing drizzle that I sent our folks home. Hopefully they could get home without any accidents. Besides, I needed to crash, and I don't mean in a car.

I had endured enough scary moments in a car that day.

It took us three hours to travel the fifteen miles from the church to our house. On the painstaking journey home, Joy reminded me how Jesus had reacted when *He* had seen other people in pain.

"If you recall," she said, trying to put a little salve on my wounded pride, "Jesus was deeply affected by other people's losses, too. Remember how He responded after His friend Lazarus died?"

I did remember. Jesus had wept, and not because He had lost His friend forever. He hadn't. He was about to raise Lazarus back to life.

She continued, "Jesus wasn't crying over His personal loss,

because He was the one who was about to make His loss found again. So I figure He must have wept because He felt the pain of those around Him."

Yep. I was sure she was right. That's what I had experienced, too. I had felt those people's pain.

"And," she said, in a mothering tone, "I figure that if it was okay for Jesus to get emotionally moved by other people's losses, then maybe it's okay for us to be affected too. Some call it *empathy*, you know."

I knew she was right, and I could tell she was on a roll, so I said, "C'mon, preach it! Let me have it. All right."

She finished her sermon by saying, "Empathy is what happens when you hurt almost as much as the person next to you. Maybe it's something God allows in His kids—people like you and me—so we know how *He* feels when *we're* in pain."

I nodded in agreement. "Amen!" It was comforting, in a small way, to know that God was crying right along with that family that afternoon. And that He weeps right along with us when we're in the middle of a serious tragedy.

She was right. If it's okay for God to empathize, then empathy must be a godly trait.

"However…" She was about to add an addendum to her message. "It's probably *not* a good idea to let that empathy cause you to lose your cool and blast off at a total stranger."

Boy, if there was one lesson I had learned from that particular detour, it was what she just said. I made a decision, right then and there, that from now on I would make it my practice *not* to scream at total strangers when those emotions were piling up and looking for a place to spill over.

It might be okay to *feel* empathy, but it's *not* okay to dump my empathy on others, at least not tall, athletic people who could punch my lights out.

I summed up our detour-filled day by saying, "You know, even though Matthew died, I'm quite sure that God did what was best for the little guy."

And I meant it. My side road to the bedside of a dying little boy reaffirmed for me that God loves and cares for His little ones more than I can imagine. It was okay for me to have prayed, "Thy will be done," because His will was best.

It always is.

On the way through the door of our mobile home, I found myself humming the chorus, "He who began a good work in you will be faithful to complete it."

As I fell into bed and turned out the light, I thought, *It sure is a good thing God doesn't give up on me. I'm sure glad He keeps building my character every time I act like one.*

It had been a long, stressful day, and yet, in a strange way, it had also been a good one. The detour from being in control, to the hospital, where I was out of control, and then to the post office, where I had lost control, had taken me right into downtown humility. It had been an exhausting journey, and yet, I was grateful for the trip.

CHAPTER NINE

The Confrontation Zone

T hose sound like pretty serious allegations to me," I blasted, only marginally aware that my voice had been raised to a near yell.

"They're not allegations. They're *facts!*" shouted back the voice on the other end of the phone.

That's when I heard an awful click on the line, and then silence. Deathly silence. The kind of silence that ends friend-ships and starts wars.

As the blood rushed from my head back down into the rest of my body, I began to realize where I was and what I was doing. I had just lost a shouting match with a respected friend, and I had just entered...the confrontation zone.

I first met Russ Collins when my family and I flew in from Texas to interview for the job at the church in Ann Arbor. I had meetings with just about every group or committee you can think of, and one of the most enjoyable sessions was with the church council, which included many of the wise, older leaders in the congregation. I was immediately taken with Russ. Joy and I both were.

His silver hair shone as if he polished it every morning. Joy, whose sweet disposition allows her to ask things I would never dare ask (and get away with it), leaned close to Russ and whispered the question right up front: "What do you do to make your hair so shiny?"

Russ lifted his head toward the ceiling and laughed his characteristic jolly laugh, straight from the diaphragm, complete with a couple of tears to wipe from the corners of his eyes. He leaned close, lowered his voice, and asked in return, "Promise you won't tell our secret?"

Joy got closer. "I promise."

"Bluing."

Joy cocked her head to one side and smiled. "That's it?"

"Yep." Russ was so tickled that she had asked. You'd have thought she'd just asked for the combination to the family safe by the way he answered her. He was as magnetically drawn to Joy and me as we were to him.

"Yes, indeed. Dorothy and I just put a few drops of bluing in with our conditioner, and that's what gives this extra little zip. D'ya like it?"

And again he laughed, heartily.

Joy grinned, took one more close look, and said, "It's great. So shiny, but not blue at all."

He bent his silver mane so she could touch it. She did, ever so gently.

"Bluing, huh?"

"Yep."

He leaned a little closer, like a father telling his kids to go to sleep so Santa can come fill the stockings. "Bluing."

Russ and Dorothy had thrown themselves into the church work there as much as anyone. They had moved to Ann Arbor after he put in a stint in the service, where he had learned to do lost wax castings and other dental lab work. He opened his own business and worked long hours to ensure his customers had perfect fits with their crowns and bridges.

Russ threw himself into whatever project he tackled with the same enthusiasm and attention to detail that we had noticed at our first meeting. He asked questions nobody else thought to ask. He was determined that we would be adequately compensated so Joy wouldn't have to get a job outside the home if she wanted to stay home and raise our kids. He felt that if a guy worked hard, he ought to be rewarded. "A workman is worthy of his hire," he quoted.

"But," he added, mimicking the blustery voice of that investment broker on the old TV commercial, "that kind of reward should be made the old-fashioned way. You ought to *earn* it." He meant it, but he said it with a smile. At least he was honest. You knew where you stood with a guy like Russ.

We thoroughly enjoyed being around Russ and Dorothy. Shortly after we had moved to the area, we were invited for a Sunday lunch at their house.

Afterward, on the way home, Joy said, "She reminds me of someone. Who is it?"

"A slim Mrs. Santa," I said, reading her mind.

"That's it!"

It was uncanny. Dorothy was lovely, charming, and matronly (but not as plump as the pictures of the traditional Mrs. Santa). She kept an immaculate house, cooked a great meal, and just seemed like the type of lady in whose basement you'd find little elves—if you peeked in quickly without offering any warning.

About a year into the new job, the church was growing and we were very busy, both at church and at home. At the same time we were giving birth to several new Bible study classes, Joy was giving birth to our second child, Clark III.

We were thrilled with the church nursery, since our oldest, Katheryn, had been lovingly bounced on Dorothy Collins's knee and rocked in her special chair, the one with the squeak that put all the babies to sleep. Then she had "graduated" into Mary Kornacki's toddler class, where she was learning about all the wonderful things in nature God made for us to enjoy.

So now it was little Clarkie's turn to ride in Dorothy's squeaky chair and receive the kind of warmth and love that makes for some wonderful early imprints from church.

But about that same time in the church's history, our pastor, Paul Calmes, acting as his own contractor, began building a house for his wife and three kids. Paul, like Will Rogers, never met a man he didn't like. He had a way of putting people at ease in almost every situation. Because he didn't want to appear self-serving with the house deal, he had gone to the church council and asked for their opinion and ultimately, for their approval. They had given Paul their blessings to spend a little extra time in the summer and fall overseeing the project.

He'd been involved in two previous building projects at churches where he'd served, and had also supervised the building of at least two other houses back in Oklahoma, where he and his wife had lived.

A couple of months after Paul had begun the project, Russ began dropping some hints to me that he felt the pastor wasn't spending enough time at church. I passed them off with comments like, "Well, he does spend a lot of time at the office in the evenings, after most people have locked up and gone home. I see him putting in lots of hours that other people don't see."

I tried to cool Russ's jets by dousing his fears with cold facts. I really liked both men, the pastor and Russ, and felt we were all very good friends. At first the little comments didn't bother me, since I thought they were just Russ's way of digging for information. I figured as soon as I provided the truth about our pastor's good working habits, Russ would back off.

He didn't.

Russ began turning up the heat under his hints, little by little, until I sensed some embers smoldering under his normally cool exterior.

Since I had visited Russ in his lab and had heard him talk of how angry it made him to watch people who didn't work hard, I realized that his rock-solid work ethic might be affecting how he viewed other people's work. Yet, seeing things from his perspective, I could understand how he would feel about someone who didn't have to keep steady hours, considering the long hours Russ had worked.

He once said to me, "With a one-man lab, if you don't show up for work, the crowns don't get made. If the crowns don't get made, you don't get paid. If you don't get paid, the groceries don't get bought. If the groceries don't get bought, the family goes hungry."

I got his point.

He figured if you weren't in your office working, you must be out doing something else, like *not* working. It was as simple as that.

After a few weeks of these uncomfortable conversations, I began to feel caught in a tug-of-war between two men I greatly admired. Russ, the hardworking elder friend with a strong work ethic and a great sense of humor, and Paul, the hardworking pastor friend with flexible hours and a great sense of humor.

And I was the rope.

This detour had taken me down off the high road of warm friendships onto the bumpy, rain-rutted dirt path of a three-way conflict. And at the pace we were moving, the road seemed headed straight toward the crossroads of confrontation. A showdown, with live fire and casualties.

Not wanting any of us to be wounded, I tried squeezing a little humor into my talks with Russ in an effort to put out the fuse on a loose cannon, but the sizzle only got louder. Then I tried disarming my other fellow soldier by encouraging Paul to visit Russ once in a while, thinking that if they spent time together, Russ would see that Paul was still very concerned about his church members.

Finally, late one evening while I was working in my church office, Russ called. The friction was reaching a critical point, producing smoke, which I imagined was coming from Russ's ears. With all the tact I could muster, I tried to help Russ see that the pastor was making late-night hospital visits, holding after-hours counseling sessions, and doing early-morning paperwork, to keep up with the church load despite his time at the new house.

"You know, Russ," I said, "Paul has lived in several small rental homes up to this point. I really do think it's fair that he get a chance to build a house big enough to accommodate his family, especially with all the entertaining they do for church functions.

"And besides," I said, placing the it-will-be-over-soon card on the table, "his house will be finished in a month or two, and he can get back into full swing at the church."

He shot back, "But if he's not putting in 100 percent, it's as if he's *robbing* the church!"

Robbing? In my book, that's a fighting word.

That's when the phone call lit *my* fuse, signaling a burning confrontation between the craggy, silver-maned elder, and the young, inexperienced minister of education and music.

"You *do* recall, don't you, that Paul got permission from the church council to build this house?" My voice had lost its friendly tone by this time.

I knew the minute I said it that I shouldn't have.

It was a terrible place to be, in the middle. And wanting to defend my good friend the pastor to my good friend the elder, my emotions began a rapid elevator ride from my gut up to my mouth.

Russ retorted, "Well, I think the church council gave Paul what he wanted. I'm not sure it was the right thing for them to have done."

Not wishing to go down that road for fear I would pit the entire church council against my friend, I backtracked and suggested that the three of us meet together. "I'm sure, Russ, that if you, Paul, and I get together in the same room where we can look each other in the eye, we can work out these differences.

I know Paul cares about you and that you care about him."

No sale. Russ was thoroughly roused by this time.

He got louder.

I got louder.

When Russ said, "I think he cares more about that house of his than he does about this church," I simply couldn't agree with him. I had been on those hospital visits when Paul wept with dying people. I had seen him do things to help people that nobody else in church had seen, because he did so many of his good deeds in secret.

I knew how much the pastor cared for the church. I felt I just had to tell Russ the truth as I saw it, because for me to agree with him meant I was turning against my pastor, something that could lead to his getting fired. I certainly didn't want that.

That's when the emotional elevator reached the top floor. When the doors opened, my volume level peaked as well, and I surprised myself by shouting back at my friend.

Then came the angry click and the awful silence.

I couldn't remember when I had ever been hung up on like that. I just sat there, breathing fast and shallow. My knees were weak, and my hands shook.

With my middle fingers I rubbed my temples for a moment, wondering, *What in the world do I do now?*

The thought came quickly, with hardly any time for me to disagree.

If your brother sins against you, go and show him his fault, just between the two of you. If he listens to you, you have won your brother over.

Instinctively, I knew it was the right thing to do. To wait

and hope the whole thing would blow over would be disaster. It would only snowball, growing larger with each new behind-the-back conversation. Sides would be taken, armies would be trained, and before long, I would be wandering in the DMZ, wondering how I had helped start Church War III.

I had no idea what I wanted to say, but I locked my office door and headed to the car.

By Russ's expression when he opened his front door, I don't think he expected me to show up five minutes after our conversation. He just stood there, looking through the screen, not knowing what to say.

I spoke up, praying for the Lord to give me words that wouldn't blow the whole thing out of the water.

"Russ, I just want you to know that I'm really sorry I raised my voice on the phone."

My knees were shaking, but now that the first words were out, the rest came more easily. "I love you as a respected older brother and I don't want anything to come between us. I think our friendship is too important to let something destroy it. Can we talk?"

Whew.

I think I know how those words got into my mouth. I believe the God of all purposeful detours, through His Holy Spirit, put them there a split second before they made it past my teeth. Because I'd had no idea what I was going to say before I said it.

Russ opened the door and invited me in.

It was tense at first. Dorothy busied herself in the kitchen. She knew what had just happened.

Russ and I talked for about an hour. I tried to tell him all the ways I had seen the pastor work, even when others hadn't. I tried to encourage him to meet with the pastor and at least make his concerns known. Things weren't ironed out immediately. But we made progress.

Just before I left that night, Russ walked me to the door. "Thanks for coming over," he said. "Your friendship means a lot to me."

I replied, "Me too. I think maybe we both grew a little tonight. D'ya think?"

He grinned that wonderful warm grin of his, raised his face toward the ceiling, laughed that deep, wonderful laugh, and then pulled me into a manly hug as the warmth of restored friendship poured over us both like healing oil.

We had both just emptied the chambers of our verbal weapons.

Russ and I had several more chats, and I tried to find opportunities to involve the pastor in some of them. And several months later, after the pastor's house was finished, Paul and his wife, Barbara, hosted a Christmas get-together. By then the church had begun a building project of its own. Standing in the wonderfully decorated living room, Russ admitted to me, "He sure knows a lot about building, doesn't he? We're fortunate to have him here as our pastor...for such a time as this."

That was years ago. Since then, Russ and Dorothy have continued to treat Joy and me as though we were their own kids. We moved to another church, several miles away, but I still drive the thirty minutes to Ann Arbor once in a while to have lunch with him. He always treats; he likes German food at Metzgers downtown.

Russ called just the other day. He had bought a tape with our favorite storyteller talking about some funny things that happened in churches. He said, "I'm going to hold the phone up to my tape machine. Listen to this." And he played it. "Wasn't that great?" he said, laughing. I could picture him, with his shiny silver hair, wiping the tears from the corners of his eyes.

I did like it.

It was hilarious.

But it was even more remarkable because he called for no other reason than to share a two-minute laugh with his friend.

He said simply, "That's it. I just wanted you to hear that. I knew you'd get a kick out of it."

"Thanks, friend," I said.

And we hung up.

It's good to have detoured down the road of conflict, met at the crossroads of confrontation, and then to have found our way back onto the high road of friendship.

Mighty good indeed.

CHAPTER TEN

Horseless in Sleepy Hollow

A flash of lightning stopped me in my tracks at almost the same instant a cannon of thunder blasted adrenaline straight into my nerves. I recoiled from the deafening crack just as a ten-foot-long tree limb, big around as my leg, crashed to the ground. It splashed into the mud puddle I happened to be standing in at the time.

"This is crazy!" I said out loud, knowing that nobody could possibly hear me. The air smelled hot, as if someone had stuck a huge pair of jumper cables onto the tree next to me and cranked up the juice.

A car sped by, splashing water up onto the narrow strip of grass and mud where I was trying to walk, then swerved around the tree limb that was now blocking half the right lane of Highway 9. It didn't matter that the wall of water washed against my slacks like an ocean wave. What was a little more water? I was already soaked to the bone.

Joy had our kids, and our car, with her in Michigan, visiting her relatives, while I stayed in New York where I was working at the time. We rented the lower third of a three-story house on North Broadway, half a block off Route 9 in what was then called North Tarrytown, just a half hour train ride from New York City. Shortly after we moved, the local historical society claimed victory in a long-running battle for a town name change. From that point on, the village would be known for its older and more literary designation...Sleepy Hollow.

Since my back had gone out early in the summer, I'd been getting regular adjustments at a chiropractor in Ossining, straight up the Hudson River to our north. With Joy gone in our only vehicle, I relied completely on the excellent public transportation system to get around. On this particular day, after my 5:30 P.M. appointment, I walked the two blocks to the highway, glanced at the bus schedule, and decided I had just enough time for a quick slice of pizza at a local deli.

Unfortunately I had misread the schedule, and I watched in dismay as the last bus of the day stopped just outside the deli's front window and then headed south, toward Sleepy Hollow and my home...seven miles away.

It had been a typically muggy August day, but as I started hoofing it for home, I noticed a menacing wall of dark clouds to the west. They didn't look good. Not at this time of year, and not with the kind of violent thunderstorms we'd been having.

That stretch of highway didn't have any sidewalks, so I walked on the street itself, next to the curb. When cars approached, I hopped up onto the grass. In that manner, I covered the first four miles in about an hour.

Counting the seconds between lightning strikes and the

sound of thunder, I realized the storm was closing in. I picked up my speed, hoping I could travel the remaining three miles in better time than those clouds took to reach me.

No such luck. With two miles to go, the sky let loose with a deluge. It felt like I was standing directly under a fire hose.

The rain by itself wouldn't have been so bad, since it at least offered a respite from the heat. But the thunder and lightning became downright scary. Especially when the lightning hit that tree so close to where I was standing. And to make matters worse, it had gotten dark. Real dark.

The stage was set for my detour through the Sleepy Hollow cemetery.

What started out a year earlier as a dream job in an exciting, history-filled setting had been quickly turning into a nightmare. The funding for my job was disappearing, and though I loved the work and the people I worked with, I was faced with a decision: either stay and try to build the company back up, or leave, returning to a more familiar role as pastor in a local church.

What should I do? I walked under another tree, hoping it wasn't going to act as a lightning rod. I'd already uprooted my family not long before, and I knew another major move would demand even more major adjustments—and big-time stress—for everyone. Especially Joy. Each time we'd moved before, I'd been able to dive into the new job while she was left at home to unpack boxes and try to help the kids adjust to our new surroundings.

But on the other hand, I wasn't at all confident in my ability to get the company back on its feet. Caught in the middle of two storms, one at work, and the one on my way home, I felt like those disciples of Jesus caught in the middle of a frothing lake, with the waves growing higher and their hopes sinking lower.

Storms seem more frightening when you can't see, since you don't even know which way to go to find your way out.

Just then, two headlights approached through the gloom, slowing as they drew near. A large black Lincoln Town Car pulled up next to me. I hadn't even tried to hitchhike, since almost nobody picked up anybody this close to New York City. The passenger side window lowered a couple of inches.

I was about to thank the kind fellow for giving me a lift when he hollered, above the noise of the rain pelting the car, in a typical New York accent, "Yo, buddy! Which way to Pleasantville from here?"

I sighed, wiped water from my eyes, pointed, and said, "Down that way about a mile, then left. You'll see the sign."

His one word, "Thanks," was almost obliterated by the next thunderclap. I hightailed it across the street, thinking it might be safer to get behind the stone fence and walk the remaining mile to our street through the cemetery. The stone wall was only about three feet high at the north end of the property, so I hopped over it with ease.

Our house sat only three short blocks from the fabled graveyard where, according to Washington Irving's classic tale, the Headless Horseman galloped across the bridge each Halloween night. I had never actually seen this cranially chal-lenged fellow, and I always chuckled when people joked about how much I resembled Ichabod Crane.

Even so, it wasn't much fun finding myself in the middle of the legendary graveyard on a dark and stormy night.

What was most frightening was the unknown. My future, both in the graveyard and in my job, were completely unknown to me.

The meteorologist had warned us earlier that month to avoid standing under tall trees in the event of a thunderstorm. That was impossible in this part of Westchester County, where nearly every tree was as old as Washington Irving, and therefore very tall. There were very few places where there were *not* tall trees.

Gathering my wits about me, I did what any faith-filled person would do. I ran like the dickens, zigging and zagging my way around two-hundred-year-old tombstones. Lightning flashed and I read a familiar name on one of the grave markers. VanTassle. I recalled from my earlier (and more peaceful) strolls through the cemetery that Washington Irving had actually roamed these hillsides gathering names for his characters.

Spying the Old Dutch Church in the distance, I made a beeline for it, remembering that a large, ornamental iron gate stood at the cemetery's entrance just below the church. If I made it to the gate, I would be only two streets and four minutes away from my dry, safe home.

Not being a superstitious person, I was more afraid of being struck by lightning than I was being struck by the Horseman's sword. But I ran just the same.

Arriving out of breath at the entrance, just down the hill from the old church, I tried the gate. Locked. I stood for a moment, looking around, wondering which way to go to get out of this place now that I was in it.

I felt as trapped in that graveyard as I did in my current job situation.

Lord, I said aloud to the storm, *I sure could use some direction.*

I really meant it.

Not wishing to cross a small stream that was becoming a larger stream, I opted to backtrack a little, up the hill to the other side of the church. There I found a small break in the iron spears protruding from the cemetery's rock wall. I scaled the four-foot-high wall, wondering what people would think if they saw me emerging from the graveyard on a night like this. Grabbing hold of the iron bars at the top, I breathed a prayer that the lightning wouldn't decide to ground itself at that moment.

It didn't, and I hopped safely down to the sidewalk below. With very little energy left to jog, I simply walked to the corner and then up the hill toward North Broadway and our house.

Since Joy and the kids were gone the house echoed with emptiness, and I suddenly felt as drenched with loneliness as I was with rain. After changing into some dry clothes, I sat down at the kitchen table. My Bible was open to the Psalms, where I'd been reading earlier that day.

Without anyone to talk with about my lack of direction, I knew I had to make a decision soon. If it was time for a change, I would have to let the board of directors know, and I would have to search for a new place of service, hopefully in time to get our oldest daughter enrolled in school. My three-week window of opportunity was closing fast.

Exhausted from my run through Sleepy Hollow and from several nights with very little sleep, I poured my heart out to the One who had been there with me all along.

God, I cried, *I've reached the end of myself. I don't have anything left. I can't decide what to do. I can't do this anymore by myself.*

And I broke down and sobbed.

My own personal cloudburst drenched the page of my Bible, upon which was printed Psalm 34. Through a haze of tears, I read a few of the verses:

I sought the LORD, and he answered me;
he delivered me from all my fears.

I chuckled and thought, *Well, Lord, You did just bring me safely through the cemetery.*

Then I read verse 18, where David had written, "The LORD is close to the brokenhearted and saves those who are crushed in spirit."

At that moment, something happened—something so strange I cannot fully explain it. All I know is that God Himself, through that verse, spoke more loudly than the loudest thunderclap I had just heard.

It was as though He said, "I'm glad you are at the end of yourself. Now I can start doing My work in your life."

I began to weep again, but this time with tears of joy. I felt the warmth and peace of His presence flood over me, head to toe. He might as well have appeared in person and said, "Peace, be still," because the storm calmed at the instant I read that verse. His presence in that room was palpable.

For nearly five minutes I cried, almost uncontrollably, filled with the unmistakable sense that everything was going to be okay. I thanked Him out loud, over and over again, and then got up from the table, washed my face, and made supper.

Nothing about my circumstances had changed. I still hadn't made any job decisions, but my attitude had been completely overhauled. It would be okay now. I knew it would. Because God was in charge.

Before I turned in later that night, my decision came easily. I would write the letter tomorrow, letting the board know I was leaving. I thanked God again for His incredible peace, turned off the light, and enjoyed my best night's sleep in weeks. I awoke refreshed and with the sense that God had a place for me back in Michigan, where Joy's family lived. I knew it had to be Michigan, even though it wasn't clear yet where that would be.

Later that week I recommended to the board that they hire our administrative assistant to fill my position, at least until they could get back on their feet. Without my salary package, the current income would be sufficient to keep the office going for at least another year. Some board members balked at my leaving after only a year, but I knew it was the right thing to do. (The company is still going strong to this day, thanks to the capable leadership of that administrative assistant who later became the director.)

In less than a week, I received a phone call from Richard Rogers, a fellow we call an "associational director of missions." His ministry role involves helping a number of churches in southern Michigan. He had just received one of the résumés I had sent the day after I wrote my letter of resignation at the current job.

"You'll never guess what happened," he said on the phone.

"Try me," I answered.

"A church in Adrian recently called a man to be their pastor. He was all set to come. They'd even lined up a series of meetings—so he could preach right after he got there. But just today, at the last minute, he called and said the Holy Spirit had told him he wasn't supposed to come after all."

After the events of the past week, I wasn't surprised.

He continued, "Would you be willing to talk with some of the search committee members on the phone?"

"Sure."

"Tonight?"

"You bet."

"Okay. I'll have them call you in an hour or so."

If you've ever been on a search committee, you know that searches are difficult, time-consuming ordeals. Some searches can take months. Richard's phone call took place just seven days after I had received God's promise that everything was going to be all right.

Some people might have considered his phone call a coincidence. I was at such peace about my circumstances that I knew without a doubt who was calling the shots.

After an hour on the phone with five people from Trinity Baptist Church in Adrian, Michigan, I felt almost certain that the Lord would be leading us to that church.

I was supposed to leave work in two weeks, but the committee called back and asked, "Would it be possible for you to come here in only a week? We'd still like to hold our series of meetings, and we'd like you to preach each night."

I checked my schedule, got the okay from my board to leave a week earlier than originally planned, and we plunked down a Visa card on the counter of the U-Haul rental agency, not knowing how we would possibly be able to pay back the cost of the truck. The total on the bill was $1,101.

The following Sunday, just three days before we would leave New York, our pastor called us up front at the close of the morning service. Bruce Boria, an outgoing, warmhearted man, said to the congregation, "Clark and Joy and their family have come to us by faith. They've served us while they have lived here, and they have lived by faith. Now they're leaving by faith. I think it would be appropriate for us to send them off with our love. Let's take a love offering to help them along the way."

Joy was blubbering and I was speechless. Even though we hadn't served on staff at this church, we had grown to love these people like our own extended family. We had begun a college Bible study and had enjoyed having many of the students in our home on Sunday afternoons. Our kids had gotten to be good friends with these church members' kids. This had been our real home away from home.

Watching them take that offering, we just stood and hugged each other and cried. God was taking care of us, right up to the day we moved.

After the service, the chairman of the deacons walked up to us and handed us a huge wad of bills and checks. He said, "Guess how much is there."

"Oh, I couldn't," I stammered, embarrassed.

"Nah. Go ahead. Guess how much." He was insistent.

"I dunno. A couple hundred?"

"Higher." He grinned.

He was making this a game, and I was already so humiliated I just wanted him to tell me and get it over with.

"Five hundred."

"Higher."

I decided to get it over with and shoot way over the top so I could narrow it down somewhere in the middle.

"A thousand."

His grin grew even larger. "Higher!"

"You're kidding."

"Nope. I'm not kidding. Would you believe it's 1,100 dollars?"

I wanted to say, "Well, actually, yes. I *would* believe it. Because God promised me a couple weeks ago that everything would be okay." But I didn't. Instead I just said, "Wow."

Another impish thought crossed my mind. I thought about looking up to heaven and saying, "Well, God, looks like You're a dollar short because our U-Haul bill is 1,101 dollars." But I didn't dare say that either.

We just stood there, shaking our heads.

Three days later, as we hopped into the cab of our loaded truck, ready to wave good-bye to our dear church family in Tarrytown, Joy reached into the pocket of her sweater looking for a tissue to wipe her good-bye tears. Her sister had given her that sweater a year earlier, and it had been hanging in the closet, unused.

Instead of a tissue, she pulled out a crumpled one-dollar bill.

My detour through the graveyard of an unknown future revealed to me that God is not frightened by the unknown. He's not intimidated, because He knows everything. He knows every detail of my future, including—*right down to the dollar*—how He's going to provide for it.

All I had to do to find God's direction for my future was to give up trying to figure it out by myself. I came to the end of myself. And when I did, there He was, in the middle of my detour through Sleepy Hollow, waiting patiently at the end of my rope.

CHAPTER ELEVEN

The Note

Thereʼs just not enough of me to go around," I told Joy, hanging up the phone after yet another barrage of bad news.

It had been a difficult holiday season, including a series of tragedies among our friends. I was wrung out, and the human question arose, *Am I really doing anyone any good?*

Normally upbeat and optimistic, Joy and I had both begun slipping off that high road onto one that ran through the bog of self-pity and negative thinking.

It wasnʼt any single person or event that had pulled us off the straight and narrow. Rather, it was a lot of little things that caved in on us like too much snow on a roof. One couple told us their marriage was falling apart. We had visited three people in the hospital, and felt their pain. A young lady had shown up on our doorstep late one night, crying her heart out. Joy had tried to console her as she sorted through the crazy quilt of a love life. A few weeks earlier we'd attended the funeral of a friend who'd died from cancer. She was only five years older than Joy.

So many needy people. So many demands. So many crises. Yeah, that was the ministry, we weren't naive about that. But this was getting ridiculous. We began to feel like a power outlet with too many extension cords plugged in, draining off our energy.

"Chris is back in jail," I told Joy, explaining the phone call.

"Again?"

"Again."

Joy shook her head. She was as burned out as I was. Seems like each time we took our eyes off the One who knew our future, we started to sink below the surface of our stormy surroundings.

Intellectually, I knew that helping others always brings its own reward, maybe not here on earth, but eventually. And my mind knew that I wasn't working for "rewards," anyway. Ideally, I was helping others simply because I was being obedient to Christ. That was reward enough.

But my emotions have been known to lie to my intellect. Those particular emotions were whispering, *Nothing you do really matters.*

I had tried to help a young man make better decisions and he turned up in jail...again. I had tried to help a grieving friend, but he was still sad. I had tried to save a couple's marriage, but they were still separated.

God just hadn't answered my prayers the way I wanted Him to! (Terribly selfish, I know, but putting too much emphasis on that word *self* in the term *self-pity* only sinks you deeper into the quagmire.)

I sat on the couch, watching our three kids decorate the tree. They asked if I wanted to help them set up the manger scene and I just sighed, forced a smile, and said, "I'm enjoying watching you guys do it this year. Go ahead." Even the Chicago Brass playing "Joy to the World" on the stereo couldn't keep me from sinking deeper and deeper into the swamp.

We heard a thump against the wall. Katheryn said, "Mail's here." She recognized the sound made when the carrier dropped the mailbox lid after she deposited the newest batch of junk mail and bills. She and Callie ran to retrieve the mail while Clarkie adjusted the livestock in the manger scene.

"Wow, look at this one." Katheryn held up a particularly colorful, hand-decorated envelope. We had received lots of store-bought Christmas greetings that week, but this card had obviously taken some real, honest-to-goodness artistic effort. The pen and ink designs were magnificent. And the calligraphy! It was superb.

I flipped it over to see if the clever sender had included a return address. The back was adorned as beautifully as the front, including a couple of vivid stickers to hold the flap in place.

Noting the name on the back, I stopped in my tracks. I cast my eyes to the ceiling and said, "Ho boy."

"What?" my kids asked. "Who's it from?"

"Man," I said, "I hope to goodness he's not needing a place to crash this holiday season."

"Who? Who?" the kids chimed in. I still hadn't answered their question.

"Bertrand..." I said flatly.

Clarkie asked, "What kind of a name is *that?*"

I removed a beautiful card, obviously hand-drawn with colorful markers. Bertrand had always been very artistic. He had also been a drunk.

"Who's Bertrand?" all three sang in unison.

I'd been so preoccupied with the card and the neatly folded letter inside, I'd kept my kids in a state of curious frustration.

"Uhm," I said, still staring at the card, hoping against hope that he wasn't coming to town. "Bert Thompson's a guy we knew back at the church before this one."

Not a very detailed explanation, but the kids, who had grabbed the envelope with all the pretty pictures and stickers, were satisfied with the answer. They didn't remember him, and that was okay. At least the guy had sent the neatest envelope in the world.

They filtered off into the living room to look at the card while I stood, afraid to open the letter for fear it meant our high-maintenance friend would burst back into our lives again, plugging his battery cables into our energy level like so many others. I just knew how the letter would start: "Had a little trouble with the law, need a place to stay. Would it be possible...?"

"So, Bert's back, huh?" Joy came out of the kitchen wiping her hands on a dish towel. I heard in her voice the same fear that had been in mine when I spoke his name a moment earlier.

"Yeah. Hey, you don't suppose we could get an unlisted number by, say, *tomorrow,* do you?"

It was terrible to think that a man of the cloth and his wife could both be so cotton-pickin' afraid of getting in touch with one human being. I thought to myself, *Oh, dear God, forgive me for feeling this way, but I just don't know if I have enough patience and energy to deal with this guy again. Isn't there someone else available to take on this assignment?*

Back at the other church I'd invested hours with Bertrand as he struggled to free himself from the powerful grip of alcohol. What was so frustrating with him was his potential. He was one of the most intelligent and engaging personalities I knew—when he was sober.

A powerful communicator, he could talk philosophy, theology, music, you name it. I remember thinking, *What's not to like about this guy?* after his wife Karen had told us about his "bad side."

When we were first introduced, I really warmed to him. He said, "Call me Bert. All my *good* friends call me that."

"Okay, Bert," I said. "I'll take that to mean we're going to be good friends."

He slapped me on the back. "You betcha," he said. We laughed together, told a few jokes, and bantered around some old theme songs from our favorite cartoon shows back when we were kids. This guy had an uncanny memory. He could recite lyrics from songs he had learned years earlier. And he could quote Scripture better than many preachers.

But he also had a problem with alcohol, a fact I discovered only a couple of weeks after meeting him.

The pastor and I had driven over to Karen and Bert's house to see why she was so distraught. After ten minutes of letting her settle down, she sobbed, "Bertrand came home drunk *again*. He's only had this job for two months. I can't count how many jobs he's held and lost. He just won't stay sober."

This time, though, she had told him she wasn't going to let

him in the house. She locked him out and told him to come back when he was dry.

She shook as she said, "He found a piece of two-by-four and started whacking it against the side of the house, threatening to break the sliding glass door. He was so out of control. Worse than I've seen him in a long time. He said he was going to—"

She broke down in painful sobs as she explained what he'd said he would do to her. She called the police. When they showed up, he was gone. "He's out there...somewhere," she told us. "Probably sleeping in a gutter or under a bridge. He may get arrested again, and—I almost hope he does. I just don't think I can take any more. I can't keep living this way."

That was only one of many such occasions when we heard from Karen about what Bert was like when he wasn't sober.

The pastor arranged for him to work at our church on the building project for a few months, under the strict condition that he remained free of booze. The rule was, if he stepped foot on the property and we even thought he smelled like alcohol, we would tell him to go home—difficult and unpleasant as that task might be. Tough love isn't just tough on the one being loved. It's tough on everyone involved.

The arrangement worked well for a few weeks, and Bert and I worked together on the new building, listening to some of our favorite music on a boom box and swapping stories. I began to think he might have found the one place where he could stay clean and become useful.

But then one Thursday, when I was the only staff member at church, Bert showed up late for work with fifty-proof breath. I sighed, shook my head, and said, "I'm sorry, Bert, my friend, but I'm afraid you'll have to leave."

"Bertrand!" he spat out, spraying me with saliva. "Don't ever call me Bert!" He tried to poke his finger into my chest but lost his balance, grabbing the doorjamb to keep from falling over. "Only my *real* friends call me that."

"C'mon, now. I'm your friend, too, Bertrand," I said, in as calm a voice as possible. I was trying very hard to keep from showing how nervous I really was. He was actually quite a bit bigger than I, and after hearing Karen describe his angry episodes, I was quite sure he was capable of taking me down.

"Oh yeah?" he said, teeth together, eyes blazing. "Well, if you were my *real* friend, you wouldn't be kickin' me out onto the street, now, would you? You do know it's cold out there?"

It wasn't worth the effort to reason with him. I had tried so many times before and finally realized there's no reasoning with a drunk. I decided to simply stand my ground and get it over with.

"You'll have to leave, Bertrand," I said sadly. "That was our agreement."

He slurred, "Yeah, right. The agreement. Ha. You guys and your agreements. You're all the same. Nobody understands. Nobody. That's okay. That's just fine. If you want me to leave, I'll leave. But *you* can't deal with me either. Nobody can. Nobody's strong enough to know how to handle ol' Bertrand."

He had the extraordinary ability to speak the truth, about others and about his own pitiful condition, even when he was falling down drunk. He was absolutely right. I *didn't* know how to handle him. I'd tried everything I knew and then some. Nothing seemed to work.

He spewed a few other choice comments on the way out the door, and I went back upstairs to calm down and try to get some work done. Later that afternoon when I was locking up, I saw a small rock placed just inside a corner door in the basement. The rock had kept the door from shutting all the way. I also smelled beer.

I closed my eyes, took a long, deep breath, and let it out fast. Bert was back. The question was, Where?

I went searching, asking myself, *Where would I go if I didn't want anyone to find me?* My eyes landed on a closet door in the fellowship hall—the closet that took a ninety-degree turn and got smaller as it led under one of the stairways.

When I opened the door, the stench nearly drove me back. I'd found him, all right. There was good old Bert, passed out under the stairs, with his feet sticking out where I could see them from the doorway. Next to him was a half-finished tall one in a brown paper bag.

At that moment I was so mad I wanted to sober him up just so I could smack him and yell, "I have reached the end of my caring!" But instead I called the police, as the pastor and I had agreed to do as part of our contract with Bertrand.

As they hauled him off, I thought, *Lord, what's it going to take? We've done everything humanly possible. We can't do any more. Please do something to reach this guy. Please, Lord.*

I wanted so badly for Bertrand the drunk to become Bert the success. Bert the family man. But it seemed for every two steps forward, he would take three back. Maybe the reason I got so mad at this fellow was because, strangely enough, I still liked him.

If he'd been some filthy drunk in the gutter the first time I met him, then maybe I could have built a wall of prejudice to keep him at arm's length. But this guy was my friend. We'd shared some good times together. And we'd weathered some storms together, too.

I had been with him in court when they hauled him away through the back door, without even enough time to say goodbye. I had prayed with him when he had wept and cried and slobbered all over himself, promising to get better. I had been there when his wife left to stay with her mother, and I had talked him into going to a treatment center so he could get his family back.

The reason I had invested so much of myself into this guy was because I honestly thought he was worth saving. He was a precious human being, and as my father had been in the habit of saying, "This one deserves a shepherd, too."

That was the last time I saw Bertrand. That was my last memorable mental snapshot, his legs sticking out from under the closet stairway, and that stinking bottle in the paper bag. I was the one who called the police so they could come take away my friend. Not exactly a great farewell party.

That's why, when I opened that envelope, I was afraid to read the letter inside. I didn't want to find out what kind of trouble he was in now. I was afraid he had tracked us down through mutual friends. That had been his pattern. He would use up all his other friends' patience and then circle back around to some old friends who had forgotten just how much trouble he really was. I just knew he must be making the rounds again.

It had been four years since we had heard anything about him. But now, through this note, he had suddenly reappeared in our lives. Joy peeked over my shoulder, as curious as I was.

For her sake, I read out loud: "Dear Clark and Joy."

The writing on the page was artistic; he'd always had beautiful penmanship. But what in the world did he want from us?

"I've been clean and sober now for forty-four months. I'm finishing a degree in biology so I can teach high school. I'm a wounded healer, helping lead an AA group in my church."

Neither Joy nor I could believe what we were reading.

"I just wanted you to know that I haven't forgotten all the times you prayed with me and agonized over my problems."

I had to stop a moment because my voice was about to stop working. Joy put her hand on my shoulder. I took a deep breath and continued, "I know I caused you two a lot of pain, because it was obvious…

"Oh, honey," I said, ashamed of what I had thought when I first saw the envelope.

"…obvious you genuinely cared about me."

"Can you believe this?" Joy asked.

I tried my best to get through the rest of the letter without completely breaking down.

"Thanks for the time, effort, and care you invested in my life. Though you didn't see it when you last saw me, your efforts really did pay off. Well, actually, it was God who did the work (but of course you know that). However, you were His instruments used to play a healing tune."

A *healing tune.* I shut my eyes for a moment, collecting my composure, wishing I could take back all the terrible things I'd just thought about him. Joy, seeing that I was rubbing my eyes, finished the note for me.

"I just thought I'd drop you a line to let you know how

very much your care means to me. With God's great love and my grateful appreciation, Bert."

We just stood there holding the note and shaking our heads. Neither of us could speak. At the bottom of the note was a carefully penned postscript:

Enjoy your Christmas. It's His season.

He was right. It was *His* season. Despite all the bad stuff happening around us, we could enjoy the Christmas season.

One little note of encouragement—one perfectly timed little letter from an unexpected source—arrived with a clear message: Doing the right thing is always its own reward. I had forgotten that, until Bertrand's note brought me back to my senses. It took some good tidings of great joy sent by a recovering drunk to yank me out of the bog of self-pity and set me back on the road to optimism and goodwill toward men.

I had been feeling sorry for myself because I was using the word *I* too much. *I* couldn't save anybody's marriage. Only God can do that. *I* couldn't keep anybody out of jail. I could only point them to the One who could. The fact is, what sent me deep into the bog was my stubborn attempts to do God's job for Him. Something He neither desired nor expected.

I resolved at that moment to simply help others as God directed me to, and to leave the outcome in His capable hands.

God gave me an early Christmas gift. He gave me back my Christmas spirit, wrapped in a carefully penned note from an old friend. My feeble efforts of caring for a drunk over four years earlier were hurled back like a caring boomerang, smacking me between the eyes and reminding me that it's not the visible results that matter.

What matters is just doing the right thing. Caring, despite

the visible outcome. Loving people in Jesus' name and for His sake.

I started humming along with the tune on the stereo, "O come, all ye faithful," and grabbed a little tinsel to help put the finishing touches on the tree.

"Do you know what we just got in the mail, kids?" I asked.

"What, Daddy?"

"A little glimpse of heaven."

The kids just laughed.

We had, too. God sent a glimpse of the kind of reward you receive when you do the right thing. Oh, and Bert? If you're reading this, thanks. Thank you for your divinely inspired note of encouragement. This time it was *you* who became God's instrument to play a healing tune. You'll never know how important that caring gesture was. We thank the Lord for you. And we're very proud of what He's doing in your life.

You've shown us a living example of Galatians 6:9, which says (as you well know, since *you* used to quote it to me), "Let us not become weary in doing good, for at the proper time we will reap a harvest if we do not give up."

You're the harvest, Bert, my good friend. You're the harvest.

CHAPTER TWELVE

A Face in a Detour

My son, almost six at the time, stood at the end of the hall, peeking into my office. Spying only the empty desk chair, he took a deep breath and then hurled his voice into the other room, projecting it with the power of an opera star at the Met.

"HEY, MOM! WHERE'S DAD?"

"Shhh. He's in the bedroom," my wife answered in a stage whisper. "He's sick. Don't wake him."

Too late.

I kept my eyes shut, listening to his approaching footsteps. I could hear his breathing, which, because of his short stature, placed his mouth right alongside my ear. I assumed, by his lack of movement, that he was simply watching me for a moment. He was trying to see if I was actually breathing. I was trying not to. Breathing made me cough. Sleeping didn't.

Right after breakfast that morning, I had felt as strong as

Samson (before his haircut). In fact, I was eagerly anticipating the Super Summer Sunday Family Picnic at which I planned to win the blue ribbon in raw egg tossing. That was one event in which being a soft touch was an asset. By midafternoon, however, egg tossing had taken on a new definition.

The Clarkster felt my forehead.

"Whew. Hot," he whispered. "Poor guy." And he left the room.

I had the flu. It had hit like a speeding freight train and left me feeling like a piece of debris lying alongside the tracks.

At that particular point in my life, the flu was a dangerous pastime. It led to thinking.

I drifted in and out of sleep. When I awoke, I wasn't pondering the Michigan weather or the planned fun at the upcoming picnic. For some reason, I couldn't settle for such mundane molehill musings. Instead, I contemplated the mountains. Grand stuff like, "How've I done in the first half of my life?"

You'd think that one measly day out of a hectic schedule wouldn't be that hard to swallow. But as I lay there, down for the count, I felt something akin to despair wrapping around my throat. It wasn't just one day I was losing. I felt as if I was losing ground for my entire future. What was this...influenza or the first rumbles of a real midlife storm darkening my horizon?

Lying flat on my back in the middle of what should have been a productive day seemed like a good time for a midcourse evaluation. Up to that point in my life—about halfway to heaven, I figured—I'd been involved in some form of ministry. But here I was, forced into another detour from a healthy work week, facing the reality that I wasn't getting any younger...or any more productive.

And as I lay there, feeling more worthless by the moment, I began to wonder, *What's the stuff in life that really matters? What have I done that's worth anything, anyway? Who really cares if I miss a day—or a year—of work?*

You know what surprised me? None of the answers to my questions—none of the most fulfilling memories—were related to *my* plans, goals, or achievements. Not one of my memories of success looked like stuff you'd put on your résumé.

In the eighteen years of career journey to that point, all the most prominent memories related to those providential "chance" relationships had been arranged, or at least allowed, by God Himself.

While tossing from side to side on my bed, I didn't recall the beautiful, state-of-the-art sanctuary with a great sound system we'd built while at the church in Ann Arbor, though that might have been included on somebody's list of accomplishments. I didn't recall the high attendance days or the best potluck suppers we'd ever hosted. Those memories didn't even make the top ten.

You know what came to mind?

A face.

Up through the fever and the jumbled thoughts and emotions, I found myself looking again at the face of Doug.

Doug...a lovable, sixteen-year-old Down syndrome boy, who went into the hospital for a routine surgery only to discover that it wasn't routine at all.

I'd been busily planning worship music for the upcoming quarter when Ted, Doug's father, called our church from the hospital.

"Do you all have a midweek service?"

Yes, as a matter of fact we did.

"I wonder how I might find my way down to the church. I could take a cab, I suppose."

I knew a church member who lived near the hospital and offered to send him by.

"Oh, I don't want to be any trouble."

He wouldn't be, I assured him.

We'd done that sort of thing before. Lots of folks came to Ann Arbor for medical reasons, and many needed a place to worship. Several of our members were poised, ready for action, and one such member swung by, giving Ted a lift to church—and an encouraging lift to his spirits.

Ted ate our special midweek meal and feasted on the Bible study for dessert. He walked into our Wednesday-night service a total stranger and left a part of our church family. That's the way it is with some folks. They're like a familiar song; they sneak right up on you and the next thing you know, you're hooked. Can't get 'em out of your head. Or your heart.

After the Bible study, Pastor Paul Calmes and I took Ted back to the hospital, where he and his wife had been taking shifts at Doug's bedside. His wife had a ready smile and neatly pulled-back hair streaked with gray. She spoke softly, not just because she was in the hospital, or because two ministers were visiting, but because she always talked that way.

"He's the last of our ten kids," she explained, patting Doug's hand. "All the rest are grown now. Moved on with families of their own." At the sound of her words, this mother's son, though possessing the body of a grown man, blinked innocently with the eyes of a child.

She touched his forehead with the damp cloth and he closed his eyes and yawned loudly. "But with Doug," she added, "we've still got our family." She tenderly wiped his perspiring forehead. Then she paused, as though pondering whether or not to speak the next sentence.

She did.

The words, "I just don't know what we'd do without him," were left hanging in the air, next to the IV machine.

On the way into the hospital, in elevator whispers, Ted had explained what was supposed to have happened. "The doctors told us it was a routine surgery, with little risk of complication. Just a disk in his neck that should have been easily repaired. But it looks as though Doug is literally worrying himself to death."

When I had first stood in the doorway, I saw what he had meant. When Doug's eyes weren't closed, they were darting back and forth from one beeping machine to another. He flinched, turning his head quickly from side to side, trying to locate the source of the pain caused by those four stainless steel screws piercing his skin, gripping his skull like a vise.

I couldn't help but wonder if he thought this place they called a hospital was some sort of cruel torture chamber. I was an adult who was supposed to know what good those contraptions could accomplish, but even to me, that ugly piece of mechanical junk appeared strangely evil.

Doug was afraid. Terribly afraid. He clung with white-knuckled fingers to his mother's arthritic hands. She had stayed inches from his face for hours at a stretch. He had been like this for nearly two days. His mother had only left his side briefly, to eat a quick bite and freshen up. She told us, "He'd be scared to death if one of us wasn't right here with him."

"Do you think—" the father paused, choosing his words carefully— "that you two could pray for Dougy?" Of course we would. We had intended to do that anyway. That's what we do.

"But…" He paused and his look into our eyes intensified. "I know Dougy is in God's hands, but…I'd really like to know if you, well, if you sense that God has any plans for Doug's healing. Physically, I mean."

I saw what he was getting at.

Ted was asking—pleading—if we possessed the kind of discernment people all wish they had at those moments. He wanted to know if God would somehow speak more directly to or through us than through the "average" believer.

We both nodded, tightened our grip on the loving father's hand, and promised we'd do all we could. I had never been given a special sign or feeling at such times. I had prayed over the sick many times in the course of my ministry; sometimes people got better, sometimes they slipped into eternity, healed for good. But I'd never had a special sense about what God was going to do.

I glanced over at my colleague. Paul had the best bedside manner of any pastor I'd ever worked with. He seemed so natural and genuine at times like these. Hospital calls tapped the deep reservoirs of compassion within this easygoing man of God.

Paul flashed a Will Rogers smile and spoke with his warm Oklahoma accent. "Hi, Doug. I'm Paul and this here's my friend, Clark. We're here to pray for you. Would you like that?"

There wasn't a hint of condescension in Paul's voice. It was pure, soothing, caring. Paul was the genuine article. Doug glanced up quickly at his mother to check her response. Her smile lines increased by another two or three wrinkles, and she nodded ever so slightly. Doug looked back at Paul, and as though on cue from his mother's subtle hint, he nodded and beamed his childlike smile. Then he squinted his eyes tightly shut, ready for prayer. It was obvious this family had prayed before. A lot.

Paul and I reached down and instinctively took Doug's hands in ours, never removing them from his mother's, just covering all of them together in our own.

"Lord," Paul began, after a deep sigh, "we know how much You love Doug and his parents—and we thank You for that great love. We know You're the great Physician, and we call upon Your healing power to help Doug recover from this surgery. Thank You, Lord."

I wanted to see a sign, hear a message, feel a tingle. Anything. I wanted in my human spirit to *will* Dougy to live. To give him at least a dozen more years with this caring couple, so they could remain a family. I wanted so badly for this young man to remain as his parents' sense of purpose on earth. But that wasn't for me to decide. And I hadn't felt or sensed anything during Paul's prayer.

It was my turn. Feeling vulnerable and powerless, I said, "Lord, You know how very much Doug needs You to be his close friend right now. Please, Lord, shower him with Your presence, and let him know that You are with him. Help him not to be so afraid, Lord. I trust that You know what's best for Doug, Your special child. Please take good care of Doug and his parents, and let them know just how much You love them. In Jesus' name I pray. Amen."

I felt maybe I had given up too early, or not prayed with enough boldness or faith. Perhaps if I had squeezed my eyes a little tighter and believed a little harder. But I reminded myself that my job was simply to entrust people into God's care, not to tell Him what to do.

I really meant what I had prayed, that I trusted God to know what was best for Doug. I really knew deep down that God loved that young man more than we could imagine, and that He would do what was in Doug's best interest. But if Doug were my child, I'm sure I would have been tempted to pray selfishly, to give God His marching orders.

I turned to catch the earnest look on Ted's face. He was searching our faces, looking for any glimmer of hope in our eyes. It was difficult to see that look and not feel that you had somehow failed in your mission. But I looked at him anyway, trying to feel what he must be feeling, trying to imagine what he must be imagining. I suspected that his heart was one beat away from breaking.

Paul didn't have the heart to tell him that he hadn't "felt" anything. He just smiled and gave a genuinely concerned look. The silence was begging for something to be said, so I spoke up softly yet candidly.

"I wish I could tell you that I had some special feeling or a word from God as I prayed. All I can tell you is that I know God knows what is best. I wish I had more to offer than that. I really do." After I'd said it, I wished I hadn't. It sounded lame. Paul had been right to just smile and say nothing.

Despite my poor attempt at encouragement, Ted thanked

me. Thanked us both. And shook our hands.

His look of concern and intensity suddenly softened. His eyes left ours and wandered up toward the ceiling. As he drew a deep breath, a quiet look of resignation replaced the look of anxiety. Doug's daddy, a man who had let us into his most personal pain, had, in that instant, just let go of Doug, releasing his earthly son into the heavenly Father's care.

I fought back tears that were creeping to the surface. We all did.

Paul wrote his home phone number on the back of his church business card and gave it to Ted. "Please call," he said. "Any time, day or night, no matter how late." He swallowed before adding, "If anything...changes."

Paul called me seven hours later, at 2:30 A.M. His voice had a weariness that went beyond the lateness of the hour.

"The family has asked if we could meet them at the hospital. Doug isn't doing well." At that hour of the morning, I knew that was Paul's diplomatic shorthand for, "Doug isn't going to make it."

"Oh boy," I said, and let out a long breath. "I'll be there in twenty minutes. Thanks, Paul." I hung up the phone, grabbed my slacks, and scraped around in the dark on top of the dresser for my wallet and keys.

Paul and I arrived in the lobby at almost exactly the same time. We rode the elevator together, knowing this could be a tough visit. He looked at me with concern. "You all right?" he asked.

"Yeah." I said. That was Paul all over. Always concerned about everyone else's feelings. I couldn't help wondering about his.

Inside the little room, at that quiet hour of the morning, all the hospital sounds seemed amplified. The gentle hiss of the oxygen flowing through the tube to the mask, the IV pump, even the sheets moving each time Doug shifted positions.

As I stood in the doorway, I noticed that Doug kept removing his oxygen mask long enough to whisper something into his mother's ear. He did it repeatedly. At first I thought, *What a patient mother. Even though she loves him, that's got to be a little annoying.*

But as I got closer and could tell what Doug was saying, I scolded myself for thinking such a thing. Each time he pulled the mask away from his face, he said in short, clipped words, "I love you, Mommy."

His voice was weak from lack of oxygen since a cruel bacteria had taken his lungs prisoner.

"I love you, Mommy," he said again. And again.

He could say that as many times as he wished.

Ted escorted us into one of those tiny hallway conference rooms to explain the situation. "He just seems to have slipped into despair. The doctors say there isn't much they can do in situations like this. He's frightened of everything they do. He's developed pneumonia, and all the procedures they try on him just seem to cause him to become even more scared. One complication has led to another. It's like a spiral with no bottom."

Paul asked, "And how are you holding up?"

Ted smiled. "Oh, I'm okay. God has given me a peace that Doug will be with Him soon. I don't mean that to sound bad. I just know that he won't have to be frightened anymore. At this point, I'm just praying for God to…"

He paused, bit his lower lip, and regained his voice.

A FACE IN A DETOUR

"For God to take him home, where he'll be at peace."

Ted suppressed the emotion that was at the edge of the spillway in all of us. And then, as though convincing himself, he added, "I'm ready for him to be at peace."

Maybe it was the medication, maybe it was the fever. I don't know. But seven years after Doug's dad spoke those words, the sights and smells of that hospital were vivid in my mind as I lay in bed, fighting the flu. Whatever the cause, I found myself crying into my pillow.

Because Doug got to me.

Doug and Ted had taught me about life, death, the caring commitment of a loving father, and faith.

We had connected.

I lay in bed remembering how, with a peaceful, long breath, Doug's young soul had slipped away into eternity, leaving a still body behind. I recalled how, just minutes after the doctor had pronounced death, *Ted pronounced life.*

He looked right into the eyes of Doug's doctor, who was almost as shaken as the rest of us, and then patted him on the shoulder, something I thought unusual at the time. Wasn't it the doctor who was supposed to console the patient?

With a voice filled with conviction, Ted told him, "I know you did everything you could. Thank you. *Really.* But, Doctor…oh, how I wish you could know the Lord Jesus Christ like Doug knows Him, like *we* know Him. I sincerely wish you could have the peace we have right now. We know exactly where Dougy is. And he's finally healed. Permanently."

The doctor was speechless.

So was I. So was Paul. We all grew a little in our faith that night.

On our way out, Ted thanked me for my ministry to him. I didn't know how to respond. I wanted to say, "Oh, but *you* are the one who has ministered to *me.*" I hadn't done much, really. I was just there. But I was there because God had me there.

Doug hadn't fallen neatly into my things-to-do list. You can't plan relationships like that. In this case, a simple phone call from a stranger at a nearby hospital was all it took to connect us. And through that "random" connection, I had witnessed the strength of someone who knew and trusted the Christ who had conquered death once and for all.

Exhausted from my midlife remembering, I drifted in and out of sleep. Then I heard him. My son.

He had crept in again. His mom, trying to let me sleep, didn't know he was there. He stood by my bedside for a few moments, just watching. Then, when the wait was too much for him, he whispered, "Dad? You all right?"

Bless his heart, the little guy was worried about me. I mumbled a faint, "I'll be okay," rattled off a muscle-pulling cough, and said, "Right now I feel pretty rotten, buddy. But just for a little while. I'll get better." And I reached up and patted his hand, which was still resting on my head. He smiled that incredible almost-six-year-old smile, the one with one side of the mouth up, one eyebrow up. His face said, "I understand, and I wish I could do something to help." He patted my head once more and left.

I don't know how many minutes or hours had passed, but the next time I awoke, I felt my son's hand feeling my forehead, again.

"You okay?"

He was just checkin'.

"Yeah. I'll be okay." I appreciated his simple touch and his two-word question. Made me feel like someone cared.

Let's see, I thought, returning to my midlife musings, *what were those things in life that were the most important?*

My son's simple, caring gestures, and my daydreams about Doug and his dad had revealed something priceless to me. The "successes" of my life up to that point weren't statistics on a résumé. Or grades on a report card.

The most important things up to that point in my life weren't things at all. They were people. People whose lives I'd been privileged to touch, and people who had touched me. *People,* I reasoned, *are the only things going to heaven.*

The events that had given me an incredible sense of purpose had very little to do with what I wanted to happen, and very much to do with what God wanted to happen.

I thought, *Every time I've helped someone in the middle of their crisis, I've been the one who's received the greatest reward.*

Feeling my son's hand on my forehead, it struck me that my little boy had been doing for me what God had been asking me to do for others. There he was, just hanging around, watching for an opportunity to do something purposeful. And then I got sick.

My detour from health, through the flu and back out again, gave him a chance to get in on the action. He was there for me. Showing that he cared. He hadn't taken a graduate-level course on six intentional, goal-oriented steps to bedside ministry.

He just cared. He just checked in on me. He just showed up.

And I'll bet that when it's *my* son's turn to make his way home to heaven, the great Lord of the universe will say, "Son, you really helped Me."

And my son will ask, "Really, Lord? When?"

And the Lord will reply, "When you visited those people in the hospital, and in jail, and when you served lunch for those homeless people, and when you mowed that widow's front yard. And when you patted your dad's forehead when he had the flu."

"Did you see *that?*"

"I did."

And my son will say, "But Lord, what do You mean I helped You? I didn't see You there."

And God will laugh, a deep, hearty, fatherly laugh, and say, "Oh yes, but I *was* there. And when you genuinely cared for those people, you were caring for Me."

And because of my detour through the flu, I'm absolutely certain of this truth: Faith is born in pain.

At least that's where I've found it.

It seems that in the first half of my life, every time I've gotten involved with people in pain, God has been there, right in the midst of the pain, offering me an incredible sense of His purpose.

People like Ted—and Doug—usually don't appear in your carefully planned schedule or on the pages of your Daytimer. More likely you'll meet them on a detour.

Thanks to a little suffering of my own, my side road through the flu, I learned (or maybe learned again) what matters most in life. The successes I'll treasure most when my life draws to a close will be the faces of people whose pain I've shared in the name and in the love of Jesus.

If that happens best on detours, then bring 'em on, Lord.

CHAPTER THIRTEEN

Stuck in a Tight Place

D ad! *DAD!*"
Good grief, now what?

I was halfway up the stairs to my little office, intending to grab some much-needed study time. Before I could reach the top, however, Katheryn, my oldest daughter, came bounding up the stairs behind me, breathlessly delivering her usual tidings of great astonishment.

"Dad!" she yelled. "There's something in our fireplace!"

In the fireplace? Nah. Couldn't be. Probably just the wind rattling that loose slate below the door.

"Come *quick*, Daddy!" My youngest daughter, Callie, had joined in the race up the stairs and was quickly gaining on us.

I sighed, stopped on the top step—only a few feet away from precious solitude—and waited for my exuberant messengers to thunder up the stairs behind me. Looking down the hall, I could actually see my computer. I was *that* close.

All I'd wanted to do was escape to my desk in the corner of the upstairs bedroom and finish the week's Advent sermons. Here was yet another distraction, heaped like coal in my stocking in this already too-busy time of year.

With a sigh, I figured the only way to get rid of this distraction was to prove there was nothing in the fireplace. Ridiculous. This was nothing more than premature visions of dancing sugarplums—or however the poem went. It was obvious the kids were not going to let me go to work until I had investigated their claims. I resigned myself to the two-minute trip all the way back down two flights of stairs to the basement, where I would open the doors and show them the empty fireplace. Case closed.

Then I could put the latest crisis to rest and get on with the business of helping people learn how to slow down, get rid of their stress, and appreciate the real meaning of the season. *Ha.* I laughed at the irony. *Physician, heal thyself!*

Somewhere between floors, our little parade picked up my son, so I arrived in the basement with three kids clinging to my pants legs like static-charged socks out of the dryer. It's amazing how they can get each other pumped up. All it takes is one false alarm and…

Good gracious, they were right. There really IS something in our fireplace. Something alive and kicking.

I saw its eye peering at me through the crack in the door panel. At my approach, I could hear the sound of claws scratching at the door.

"Well, I'll be," I said, shaking my head in disbelief.

The kids were jumping up and down, yelling, "Told you! Told you!"

Yeah, yeah. They'd told me. It's tough to be wrong when you're the parent. There couldn't be anything in our fireplace, but there was. Quickly moving past denial and into acceptance, I said, "Whatever it is, it must have had a wild ride down that chimney—what with those bends and the drop onto the smoke shelf."

"What IS it?" the kids demanded.

This unexpected turn of events was becoming curiouser and curiouser. I had heard of bats flying into chimneys—or an occasional owl. Maybe this was Dr. Seuss's grinch, out to steal our Christmas. Trying to get eyeball to eyeball with the critter, I leaned a bit closer.

"I dunno," I admitted. "I can't quite tell *what* it is."

It was too small to be a raccoon, but too large to be a bird. And that beady animal eye! It was kind of eerie. I gingerly reached my finger toward the crack in the opening to see how friendly it might be.

"D-a-a-d," Clarkie said in a shaky voice, "Dad, I don't think you should do that."

"It's okay," I told him. "I'm just going to see if it might be—you know, tame. Maybe it's somebody's cat that got up on the roof." I could feel little Callie trembling as she clung to my leg, hiding her body behind mine, only peeking out enough to see what was going on.

This was serious stuff, Dad going one on one with a mysterious invader. Truth be told, I felt a little queasy about getting too close. But hey, I'm the dad. Dads aren't afraid of anything, right? I had to make a good show of courage for the sake of the children.

Just as I began to draw near, however, the creature went

nuts—darting around, bumping into the doors, making a ghastly racket. I yanked my hand back as if I'd just stuck my finger into a light socket.

Clarkie started to say something, but I cut him off at the pass. "I know, I know, you told me. I shouldn't have done that."

Just then I caught sight of the animal's brown and bushy tail...and that gave it away. When it came back around to the door and stuck its nose in the crack, I could tell what kind of animal we were dealing with.

"It's a squirrel," I announced, grateful to be right about at least one thing.

"Whoa." All three kids spoke in unison, as though on cue.

Katheryn: "Good thing we didn't have a fire going, huh, Dad?"

Clarkie: "Can we keep it?"

Callie: "Yeah, Dad, can we...*please?*"

Dad: "Let me think about it. Okay, I've thought about it. NO!"

Like other unexpected holiday guests we've encountered throughout the years, this one required a bit of extra attention. Ah, those detours. They can certainly arrive in the most unexpected packages.

I spoke to it softly, trying to calm it down. "Sorry, friend, no room within. Anyway, you wouldn't like this place. Gets kinda warm sometimes. I'm afraid you'll have to spend the night out behind the garage, or up a tree...or wherever it is adventurous squirrels sack out.

"Look how cute it is, kids. Maybe, if it knows we're not going to hurt it, I could just reach in and gently lift it out." I thought it might calm down after its first blast of frenetic energy. But no sooner had the last word left my mouth than it began scratching about like a squirrel overdosed on espresso.

I yanked my hand back again.

"Or not," I added quickly.

I recalled a story my neighbor had told about these seemingly innocent little squirrels ripping houses apart. So what might it do to an overly forward preacher?

The kids and I considered our options:

1) We could anesthetize it with the vapors of the starter fluid we had for the old van. That stuff was basically just ether in a spray can. *Nope*, I reasoned. *With our luck we'd all go clunk on the floor with the varmint scurrying over our unconscious bodies and stealing all the nuts out of the candy dish.*

2) We could tie a garbage bag around the door area to the wood burner, open up the doors and let the squirrel run into the bag. Nix that one. It might suffocate. And besides, those plastic bags aren't very thick. Kinda wimpy. We'd end up with a wild-eyed squirrel residing in the basement rather than the fireplace. On to plan three.

3) We could cut a squirrel-sized hole in the side of a cardboard box, place the box next to the door, and gently slide up the slate on the door, creating a nifty little squirrel corridor into the box. It would be just like walking from the gantry elevator into the space shuttle.

Eureka! No vote had to be taken. When I mentioned that idea, eyebrows went up and heads nodded all around. We were of one mind, then. We just *knew* it was the right thing to do.

Clarkie took off to find a box in the attic. Katheryn ran upstairs to barricade the kitchen (in case Plan Three bombed), and Callie shook with nervousness at the top of the stairs. (Oh, she of little faith. Alas, every team has its skeptic.) Joy decided her battle station was near Callie, who needed some consolation that Daddy was not going to make some dumb mistake and send the squirrel scampering about the living room. (I wasn't sure who had less faith in this operation, Callie or her mother.)

So, with Ma in her kerchief and I in my cap, I got out the pliers and set the squirrel trap.

It took some doing, but I jiggled loose the slate from its place in the door, all the while keeping an eye on the skittish little bolt of lightning on the other side. When I got the box in place, I slid up the slate s-l-o-w-l-y—until...ahhh...ever so gently, the squirrel waltzed right into the box, just as though we'd been practicing this docking maneuver for weeks.

Sliding a piece of cardboard down to cover the hole, I took hold of the box, keeping an eye out for little squirrel appendages that might find their way out of cracks in the top. It seemed content to be still, though, and I was grateful. Because if it had started ripping around in that box, I'm not sure I would have made it to the top of the stairs without dropping it out of sheer terror.

The kids watched breathlessly, keeping their fingers crossed as I approached the side door to the house, which my son had held open, stepping well out of the way so as not to trip his old dad.

We all let out a collective sigh of relief when I stepped over the threshold and out into the open air. I walked to the backyard, set the box down on the grass, and removed the cardboard, exposing the entrance-turned-exit. We all stood across the yard, watching, waiting, wondering why the squirrel was taking so long to leave when the way seemed so clear.

After about a minute, our guest stuck its little nose out, sniffing, making that nervous little squirrel face that makes them seem so innocent and cute. It paused a moment, took about three tentative steps just outside the box, stopped, turned around to look at us as if to say, "Thanks, blokes. Top o' the mornin' to ya," and then scampered away, a bit sootier and a tad wiser for the experience.

I accepted the applause of my three appreciative children and then headed back upstairs, hoping for at least a few moments of quiet before the next detour called me away from my Advent meditations.

Finally, I found the solitude I'd been seeking. Not a creature was stirring, not even a...squirrel.

Wouldn't you just know it, all I could think about was that crazy squirrel. In spite of myself, I couldn't help but reflect on this most recent detour from my sermon preparations. *Isn't it funny,* I thought, *how, before we had rushed to its redemption, our little visitor had frantically tried to bash its way out of its dark prison inside the wood burner?* It seemed that the harder it struggled to get free, the more pain it caused itself. It was sooty black, frightened, exhausted.

In the end, he simply had to wait patiently until one who was much bigger—one who could peer into his world—could carry him safely to that larger world where he really belonged. *Hmm,* I thought, *maybe there's a purpose in this detour after all.*

I began writing the experience we had just witnessed as an illustration for the following Sunday's sermon.

"When the first Christmas took place," I mused, "many

people on earth had fallen into the dark prison of sin. The harder they tried to bash their way out of their confines, the more they hurt themselves. In fact, they could not escape. Unless a more powerful someone came from the outside, they were trapped and in despair.

"As the carol says, 'Long lay the world, in sin and error pining, till *He* appeared…and the soul felt its worth.'"

What did the Scriptures say?

For he has rescued us from the dominion of darkness and brought us into the kingdom of the Son he loves, in whom we have redemption, the forgiveness of sins. (Colossians 1:13–14)

Yeah, this'll preach, I told myself.

"All they had to do was simply relax and allow the person who was so much bigger than they were to carry them to safety in a world where they really belonged."

But you are a chosen people, a royal priesthood, a holy nation, a people belonging to God, that you may declare the praises of him who called you out of darkness into his wonderful light. Once you were not a people, but now you are the people of God; once you had not received mercy, but now you have received mercy. (1 Peter 2:9–10)

"As long as they viewed this stranger on the outside as a potential danger, they feared His presence and fought like crazy to keep Him from making them prisoners.

"Yet when they relaxed and gave up trying to keep away from the one person who could help them, they realized that His loving hand was there to guide them to safety and freedom."

Not a bad little illustration for a guy who'd been constantly interrupted while he was trying to study. As I reflected, I realized that the incident might have an application for the preacher as well. Maybe my life had become a little crazy, too. Here I was getting all stressed out because I couldn't make things work my way, when God was allowing a marvelous little detour filled with adventure—and not without humor.

Was God smiling at me just then, saying, "How did you manage to get yourself in such a squirrel cage, Clark?" Maybe He was teaching me that I needed to relax and let Him handle things, even when it came to sermon preparation and parenting. The smaller things in life. Not just the big picture.

Christmas—and life—makes more sense when we relax and allow God to guide us into freedom. Without Him, all we accomplish is wearing ourselves out and kicking up a bunch of soot.

I went home after our Sunday evening service, built a fire, kicked my shoes off, and practiced, for two hours, what I had been preaching. I relaxed for the first time that Christmas season. It felt good to be free from the frenzied expectations I had placed upon myself surrounding the event I supposedly celebrated with joy to the world and peace on earth.

Ah, little squirrel. It took Someone Bigger Than You to break into your darkness and despair. It took Someone Bigger Than You to pluck you from the ashes and bring you into the fresh air and sunlight.

And it takes Someone Bigger Than Me to handle the kaleidoscopic details of life, the responsibilities and expectations and obligations and duties that press in from a thousand directions.

What had we sung that night? *Emmanuel, Emmanuel, His name is called Emmanuel.* It was a name that meant "God with us," and brought great encouragement and joy to all who heard it.

It still is. And it still does.

CHAPTER FOURTEEN

At the Barbershop

My son dangled his feet, swinging them back and forth as he leafed through the pictures in a six-month-old issue of *Popular Mechanics*. He was at that age when boys aren't quite old enough to know that mothers aren't supposed to take their sons to the barbershop.

So he went gladly with his mom to the local hangout, where the sun streams in through the window and the things that give you purpose in life are discussed through stories of lifetimes.

Then, for a moment, his attention was diverted from the magazine. He watched, wide-eyed with wonder, as a thin-boned, thin-haired, closer-to-heaven-than-most-of-us gentleman was helped into the seat of honor by his attentive wife.

It was no small task. He was weak. She wasn't much stronger. Together, they got him as far as the step where you put your feet. He was facing the wrong way, like the guys in the old westerns who jump off the livery stable roof onto their trusty steeds—and then wonder where the horse's head went.

My son didn't flinch. He didn't giggle. He just sat, looking first at the predicament, then at his mother, then back again. His face had that "I wonder if I should get up and help" look.

He knew the difference between slapstick comedy and respect for elders. It makes a parent proud.

They got the frail fellow turned around and plopped down into the comfortable old barber chair, where he slept through most of his haircut. Then, after the nap and the trim, came the trek out of the chair. The kindly barber helped him down from his perch, into his faded cardigan, out the door, and all the way into his '85 Buick LeSabre.

Chivalry is not dead. Not yet, anyway.

Then it was my son's turn in the chair. He hopped up with little effort, his strong young legs dangling above the step where the aged gent had just recently been stuck.

It struck my wife where it strikes me—in the philosophy gland—that the young boy with perhaps seven or eight hundred haircuts to go had just climbed aboard the same chair after a man whose haircuts (to say nothing of hairs) were obviously numbered.

And the barber took just as much care with one as he did the other.

Why is it, I thought, as my wife told me her barber story, *that a pang of sadness tightens my gut at the same time my eyes glisten with a glimmer of hope?*

My wife's story of generational transitions may have hit me especially hard because my own grandfather had recently passed away. *Willard the Wise.*

Even though I thought I was prepared for the detour I had just experienced back in Arizona, I still wasn't quite ready to let him go.

If I hadn't just gotten back from preaching Granddaddy's eulogy, I might not have paid that much attention to my wife's experience with my son in a small-town Michigan barbershop. But somehow, that picture she brought home was just what I needed to hear.

It was my mother's voice on the phone that first signaled the detour.

"Your grandfather is in the hospital," she said. And then added, "And...he's not doing very well."

She let those words sink in for a moment and then began to tell the story. "He woke up in the middle of the night and realized he was bleeding, from the colon. He gathered up his sheets, pretreated them, and put them in the washing machine before awakening Grandmother." (Because of their physical ailments, they slept in separate beds.)

Eyes closed, I nodded my head. It was just like him. He was always a stickler for neatness. The guy who wanted every leaf raked off Hardcastle's Island would be the kind of guy to pretreat his own sheets before he left for the hospital to die.

"He told Grandmother, 'Honey...Katheryn' (he always called her Katheryn or Kate), 'I think it's time,' and she got up, got dressed, and they drove together to the hospital."

It was just like him not to bother anyone. Never one to panic, practical to the end, it made perfect sense for him to drive himself rather than call for an ambulance. Willard had worked persistently for years to build a strong faith foundation, reading God's words and putting them into practice. The shadow of death held no fear for him.

Besides, he was too frugal to pay for an ambulance ride.

I can almost hear him telling Grandmother in the car, "They probably charge *fifty dollars* or more just for a five-mile ride. It's highway robbery. I'd rather drive myself and leave the fifty bucks to be spent for the Lord's work."

The way my mother described their trip to the hospital made it sound more like they were on the way to a birth than a death. But then, when you think about it, I guess he *was* preparing for a birth of sorts.

I sat there in the living room holding the phone receiver, taking it all in, trying not to interrupt with too many questions. But I just had to ask a couple.

"Is he in serious pain?"

"No, the doctors don't think so, and he doesn't complain of any."

"What are the doctors suggesting at this point?"

"Well, they say sometimes when a colon starts to bleed like this—which happens in elderly folks and people who've experienced ulcers—that sometimes the body will simply heal itself. And if it does, well, then he should be okay. That could happen in a day or so, maybe two at the most…"

Her voice trailed off, and it sounded like she was starting to choke up.

"But…if not," I added, putting the pieces together, "then…"

"If not," she said, "then he will…go to heaven soon."

Mom is an incredibly strong woman, very poised and composed most of the time. (Though she *does* tend to react emotionally to warm reunions at Christmas. Oh, and I *did* see her cry that one time when she watched the Folgers commercial where the young soldier on leave sneaks into the kitchen and wakes up his parents by brewing a fresh pot of coffee. But she's not a crybaby basket-case type by any means.)

This time, however, she was really struggling. She cried a little over the phone. She tried to disguise it, but I could tell.

Attempting to stay objective for the moment, I asked another question. "Have they given him any blood?"

"Yes…" She got a grip and continued. "They've already given him two units. But—they say it's leaking out as quickly as they're putting it in."

"Oh," I answered flatly, feeling a lump form in my own throat.

"Granddaddy told them not to give him any more. You know how he is about this stuff."

"Yes. I know."

"He told them, 'If it's my time…'" She trailed off again.

"Then he's ready," I said, finishing the sentence for her.

I heard a muffled sob. "Right," she choked out.

"So basically we're in the wait-and-see mode then, huh?"

"Yes. The doctors say we should know by tomorrow morning whether or not his body will stop the bleeding. If not, he wants to be moved to a hospice care facility not too far from home."

"Anything we can do from here yet?"

I had to offer. I felt a sense of obligation, though I really didn't know what we could do from 2,200 miles away.

"No. Just pray. You know your grandfather. He wouldn't

want you kids wasting any money on a flight out here for nothing."

She was right. Granddaddy was the guy who'd amassed a small fortune by stopping along the highway to pick up nuts and bolts. "I could use that on the new bridge across the creek bed," he'd say proudly, holding up the treasure. "These things don't come cheap, you know. I'll bet you'd pay thirty-five cents for this brand new!"

I thought I knew where this conversation was leading. "Well, Mom, since we all saw him this past summer and had such a good visit, maybe we should wait to come out until…" Now it was my turn to pause and search for the right words. "Until there's a little more reason for coming."

I was trying to avoid wording it too harshly. It would sound crass to say, "We'll wait for the funeral before we fly out there." But that's really what we were deciding.

"Yes, I think Granddaddy would prefer that you wait. If…or when…that happens, we'll all need a little extra help." Neither of us wanted to come right out and say what we were meaning.

"Okay, Mom. Thanks. Oh, and Mom?"

"Yes?"

"How are *you* doing?"

Just the fact that I'd asked gave her permission to let down her guard. She wept some more, but this time without trying to hide it. "I guess," she said in a hoarse whisper, "that although I knew this time would come, I suppose I just wasn't ready for it to end this way. But I'm okay," she added, almost as though to convince herself.

Then she said, more strongly, "The Lord is my strength."

It wasn't just so many pious words. I knew that what she had just said was literally true. True for her, and true for me. It felt better to hear her say that—and made her feel better, too.

"Well, Mom? You know that we love you—and him."

"Oh, I know, honey. I know."

"And Mom?"

"Yes?"

"Would you tell him that for me? That I love him?"

"Of course."

Granddaddy died two days later. Willard the Wise had graduated to the place he had sung about all his life: "When the roll is called up yonder, I'll be there."

The roll had been called.

He was there.

I preached a portion of his funeral service, since my own father was too weak from Parkinson's to handle it. I hadn't expected the torch to be passed that way. Yet it seemed fitting, in the middle of this detour away from our normal workaday relay race into a stark, face-to-face meeting with the fact of mortality, that the baton would be passed to me.

I was the son my grandfather had always wanted. When I was younger, I was always his "Sonny Boy." His own son had died in infancy, and so my mother and my aunt were the only two children he raised. It was an honor to preach a sermon he had been writing with his life for ninety-three years.

Two weeks after we returned to Michigan from the funeral, I found myself in the same barber chair where my son had sat a few weeks earlier. I closed my eyes and thought about my wife's story. The one about my son's visit to the barber, and about the elderly gent.

As the barber snipped, my mind wandered back to the island. I thought about the leaves, the flood, and the lessons I'd learned working with that little man with a big dream, his faded pink truck loaded with boulders and determination.

I thought about the foundation he'd built. A foundation strong enough to keep an entire island from washing away when the storms hit and the floods ravaged. I chuckled to myself as the words to a familiar song floated into my thoughts: "On Christ the solid Rock I stand." I could almost hear his voice, singing those words. "All other ground is sinking sand, all other ground is sinking sand."

There I sat, waiting for my haircut, watching the barber as he carefully cut the hair of the little guys and the old guys. I felt the pangs of conflicting emotions and watched the passing of an era, all in one quiet afternoon.

I asked myself, *Why do I feel so sad, even though I know where Granddaddy is right now?*

Fred Craddock knows why.

Fred waited in his car for his wife to finish shopping. He was parked behind another car, where he couldn't help noticing the young woman in the passenger seat, weeping as if there was no tomorrow.

Fred instantly formed in his vivid imagination the sad scenario that must have resulted in the poor lady's plight. She must have endured abuse from an angry husband, probably an alcoholic, probably in a bar around the corner, getting plastered so he could stagger back and treat her badly some more. She must be sitting in the car, deciding whether or not she should grab a cab and hightail it to the safe house.

So he thought. But he was wrong.

Just about the time Fred was about to ask the woman if he could punch her husband's lights out, he witnessed a young man leading a little boy out of the barbershop next to their parked car. The man was clean-shaven and handsome, not at all the picture he'd seen in his mind. And the boy was merely a tot, with beautiful, freshly cut blond hair.

The instant the boy climbed into the car, the waiting woman hugged him as though he'd just survived cancer surgery and wept even more visibly. Then she turned to her husband, who had already slid behind the wheel. She gestured toward the barbershop. His face reddened. He shook his head. She cried some more. Gestured some more. Hugged the boy some more, kissing his perfectly proportioned toddler head.

He shrugged, sighed, and with a look of resignation, left the car, entered the barbershop again, walked over to the chair where his little son had just sat, bent down, picked up a little lock of blond hair, and then walked back outside.

If you asked the lady holding the strands of hair, "Do you *not* want your boy to grow up?" she would probably say, "Of course I do. But his graduation to his first haircut means letting go of my baby." [1]

If you asked the elderly wife with the tottering husband, "Do you want him to stay on earth like this forever?" she would probably say, "Of course not. But his graduation into his first day in heaven means letting go of my husband."

There is a time for everything, and a season for every

activity under heaven: a time to be born and a time to die (Ecclesiastes 3:1–2).

And there is a time for cutting hair.

Now it was my turn. My turn to get my hair cut. My turn to carry on some of the family traditions. My turn to console the other family members the way the older generation had consoled me. I sat, thinking about my son's visit to the barber, about my grandfather, about Fred Craddock, and about the crying mother holding a lock of hair.

And on that quiet afternoon in the local hangout, where the sun streams in through the window and the things that give you purpose in life are discussed through stories of lifetimes, I realized that God was still there, smack-dab in the middle of my detours, accomplishing His purposes. Leading the way to heaven.

For that, my friend, is His ultimate purpose.

He desires that all should come to know Him and be with Him forever. Some people discover that fact, often in the middle of their detours. Others miss it, even though He's been there all along, trying to get their attention.

I was sad my grandfather was gone. But I was happy I would see him again when the roll is called up yonder. God's presence in the middle of my detour made it possible for me to look forward to that day. It is God's presence, you see, that makes even the most difficult of detours purposeful.

It had been a long road from my trip to the hospital with the Tin Woodman in the back of the pickup. And I had discovered that, like Dorothy, searching for a place of purpose, it had been right there under my nose all along.

Just before he died, Granddaddy had mused, "This earth's

a nice place to visit, but...heaven's my real home." Remembering that, I was able to relax in the barber chair. I thought to myself, *There's no place like home. There's no place like home.*

But sometimes it takes a few detours to get you there.

1. Adapted from a story by Marshall Shelley, *Leadership* 8, no. 4 (fall 1987): 3.

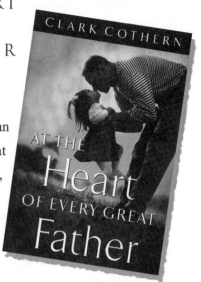